First Light

First Light

By Carolyn Gilliam

GGG Publishing

© 2013 Carolyn A. Gilliam

ALL RIGHTS RESERVED
No part of this publication may be reproduced, stored in a retrieval system or transmitted in any way by any means – electronic, mechanical, recording or otherwise – without prior permission of the copyright holder, except as provided by USA copyright law.

All scriptures are taken from the Holy Bible, English Standard Version

Cover picture: Sunrise over the Red Sea at Elat, Israel, 2006.
Photographer – Carolyn Gilliam

Website: www.carolyngilliam.com

ISBN 978-0-9833873-3-6

First Edition
Printed in the United States of America

Dedication

This book is dedicated to Miss Esther Benedict and all of the high school English teachers who encourage their students to take their creativity beyond convention. These teachers are unsung heroes nurturing aspiring young authors who will assure a future of challenging literature for the reading public.

Acknowledgements

The writing of this book would not have been possible without the assistance of a number of kind people, but first and foremost, it is the result of the constancy of my Lord and Savior, Jesus Christ, who lived the event and provided the inspiration for this work. With all my heart, I thank Him for enabling me to get into each character's life as it was on the day of their deepest despair and the privilege of discovering their wonderful joy as the truth of God's love shone through the darkness.

The seed that was planted by my friend, Sandy Gregory, took root in the fertile ground of Bible study I have participated in over the years. Now it has flourished and flowered. Kim Westfall and Alice Goldfarb edited the drafts, pruned and shaped it. Kim Westfall then repotted it in a striking cover. Many others have contributed with suggestions and enthusiasm. I honor each of them with my heartfelt appreciation for all of their efforts.

Table of Contents

Prologue . . . 9

Part I – Day of Darkness

Simon Peter, the Rock . . . 15
John, the Beloved . . . 33
Andrew, the Gatherer . . . 41
Matthew, the Tax Collector . . . 49
Simon, the Zealot . . . 59
Mary Magdalene, the Rescued . . . 73
Nicodemus, the Pharisee . . . 91
Mark, the Seeker . . . 101
James, the Brother of Jesus . . . 111

Part II – Day of Light

Dawn . . . 123
Morning . . . 135
Evening . . . 151

Epilogue . . . 159

Poem – First Light . . . 166
Scripture References . . . 169
Bibliography . . . 171
About the Author . . . 173

Prologue

John 3:19-20
And this is the judgment: the light has come into the world, and people loved the darkness rather than the light because their works were evil. For everyone who does wicked things hates the light and does not come to the light, lest his works should be exposed.

Perfect day for the beginning of the most joyous celebration in the Jewish calendar – Passover! Brilliant blue sky – refreshing breeze – Jerusalem, the capital city gleaming like a precious stone across the valley – birds joining the singing voices of the people – palm branches waving in salute to the Man the crowd expected to become king! There He is! Riding on a young donkey down a road covered by palm branches with cloaks laid down to exalt Him. Strange – the Man's smile does not reach His tearful eyes. Only He fully understands where this colorful, happy procession is leading.

As He approaches the descent, He pauses a moment before continuing down the Mount of Olives, past the bent, gnarled olive trees and the whitewashed tombs. The road crosses the Kidron Valley to the Beautiful Gate in the eastern wall of Jerusalem, the gate that opens onto Temple Mount.

For Him, each step the donkey takes has special meaning – not even His disciples understand. Who is this Man – this Jesus – the Messiah? He seems to be an itinerant rabbi traveling mostly through the villages of Galilee and to Jerusalem for feast days. But He does more than teach about a loving, redeeming God; He demonstrates this characteristic through miraculous healings of the blind, the lame and the demon-possessed. Many of those who hear His teaching and witness His miracles believe His claim to be the Son of God – but others don't.

Most notably among the skeptics are the religious leaders, the priests, the Pharisees, the Sadducees, who comprise the Sanhedrin, which is the ruling body of the Jewish people. For the past two years, these men have been very closely watching Him, baiting Him with difficult questions in an effort to find a charge to bring against Him so that they can put an end to His radical teaching. He has side-stepped every snare they have laid for Him. And everywhere He has gone, the people flock to Him in increasing numbers.

Watching the crowds around Him grow, the High Priest and his cohort have decided that they must stop this movement before it can become a threat to their power. Caiaphas, the High Priest, pointed out to them that it was better for one to die than for the whole nation to be lost. Their biggest problem was how to accomplish this endeavor without inciting the Man's followers.

A few days later, as if trying to help them, Jesus fans their animosity into hatred when he interrupts His teaching in the Temple and purposely strides to an open area of the temple grounds where business is being conducted. Some men are changing the money of Jewish worshippers from other parts of the world into the shekels which are required to pay the temple tax. Others are selling livestock to those who need unblemished animals to offer as sacrifices. It is commonly known that the transactions made in the Temple are much more costly than elsewhere.

Grabbing a whip hanging on one of the animal confines, Jesus opens the door of the pen, releasing the animals it holds. He continues until all of the animals and birds are freed. Then he goes to the tables of the money changers. Upending them, flinging coins everywhere, He angrily shouts, "It is written, 'My house shall be called a house of prayer,' but you make it a den of robbers". Chaos erupts as bystanders scurry to escape the sheep, goats, cattle and birds. The money changers grovel after the scattered coins.

The High Priest and his co-conspirators are now desperate to rid themselves of this Man forever. The opportunity for retribution comes in the form of one of His followers offering to place Him in their hands. Their plan is executed perfectly. The informant leads a detachment of temple guard to a secluded place where the arrest is made.

Immediately, Caiaphas convenes a meeting of the Sanhedrin. An illegal nighttime trial is held and Jesus is found guilty of blaspheme, but this charge does not warrant a death sentence by Roman standards. A new charge that will bring about the desired end is concocted.

The next morning, Jesus is brought before the harsh Roman proconsul, Pontius Pilate, who tries every way he can to avoid pronouncing the death sentence – even offering to set Him free. The priests lead the crowd in calling for the release of a notorious murderer, Barrabas, instead. Pilate publicly washes his hands of the matter and bows to the demands of the Jewish court.

After He is scourged, Jesus is crucified by the most heinous method of death the Romans have devised. No one defends Him and only His mother and one disciple are at the foot of His cross.

Where did the rest of His disciples go? Does anyone mourn for Him? How will His death change things? Who is He? What will become of all of who have believed in Him?

Part I
Day of Darkness

Isaiah 42:16
And I will lead the blind in a way that they do not know, in paths that they have not known I will guide them. I will turn the darkness before them into light, the rough places into level ground. These are the things I do and I do not forsake them .

Simon Peter, The Rock

Matthew 16:18-19
And I tell you, you are Peter, and on this rock I will build my church, and the gates of hell shall not prevail against it. I will give you the keys of the kingdom of heaven, and whatever you bind on earth shall be bound in heaven, and whatever you loose on earth shall be loosed in heaven.

He heard the angry crowd in the streets yelling "Crucify Him! Crucify Him!" He was afraid that they were calling for Jesus' death, but he couldn't force himself to go again to His defense and he just couldn't watch the events that seemed to be unfolding. *I am so ashamed,* Peter thought. *I don't understand why I did what I did.*

Jesus had admonished him when, with a combination of fervor and fear, he whipped out his long fisherman's knife and swung it at Malchus, one of the high priest's servants who was with the guards sent to arrest Jesus. I *didn't intend to cut off the ear. It just happened in the confusion of the moment.* Jesus had reached down and picked up the severed appendage. Calmly He replaced the ear on the man's head and healed it! Peter had stepped away from his Master in that moment. *Why did I leave Jesus at that critical time? How could I have abandoned the Master when He needed me the most? But that was just what happened! Why?*

Peter had always been a leader. He had obtained his own fishing boat soon after his bar mitzvah and had trained his younger brothers how to fish from it. They remained as his crew to this very day. He was known by all the fishermen on the Sea of Galilee as the one to go to if they needed something. Not that he did everything himself, but he always knew how to solve their problems or where to direct them to get whatever they needed.

He was a good provider for his household, which included his wife, their four children, his mother-in-law and three younger brothers. Their solid house in Capernaum was the only place they had ever lived. He attended the synagogue school and, although not the top scholar, his natural tendency to lead had emerged. He had been the acknowledged leader of His followers, too. Yet, he had not been a leader when he faced the most critical night of his life – the night they arrested Jesus! Why?

He thought back to the day he first saw Jesus. He had taken his younger brother, Andrew, and Andrew's best friend, John, the younger son of his fishing partner, Zebedee, to Jerusalem for the observation of the Feast of Unleavened Bread. This was one of the feasts which required a man's presence in Jerusalem.

Because the Jews considered the Samaritans an unclean race, Galileans rarely traveled the most direct route to Jerusalem through Samaria. Instead, they took the longer route, crossing the Jordan River and going through Perea. So, after observing the feast in the Temple, the trio traveled the Jericho Road with a large group of pilgrims who had also celebrated the feast in the capital city. In doing this, they avoided the danger of falling victim to notorious robbers who infested the route.

As they descended to the verdant valley of the Jordan River, they saw the opulent winter palace that King Herod had erected outside Jericho. Bypassing the city, they headed directly to the ford across the Jordan River. As the men walked into the water, John suddenly stopped and pointed upstream.

"Look, there he is," shouted John.

"Yes," Andrew agreed and, turning his head back, he called to Simon (for at that time Peter was known as Simon), "We are going to see the man known as John the Baptizer. Do you want to come?"

"No," Simon replied, noting the position of the sun. "Don't be too long. Rebecca is expecting us home and she will worry if we are late. I'll wait here."

When he reached the shade of a tree, he sat down. *It has been a long trip and there are still two days' journey ahead of us. I am anxious to get home to Rebecca and the children. Rebecca is a good wife and mother – everything God made a woman to be. Esther, my eldest, is now nearly a woman. All too soon some young man will be taking her to wife. She is delightful to the eye and already adept at household duties, although still under her mother's strict tutelage.*

Next is Abram, who will soon be old enough to join us on the fishing boat. It is good a thing that I have a business for him to work in, as he is not a dedicated student, doing only enough to fulfill the rabbi's barest requirements in synagogue school. Eli is just starting synagogue school. He is like a bright ray of sun – so full of energy and lively curiosity about everything that touches his life. The youngest is Deborah – sweeter than honey in the comb. She snuggles close to me when we take midday rest. She is the light of my life!

I miss the fishing, too, even though there have been many nights when the catch was so poor that we would have been better off to have stayed at home. At least we would have been more rested, he thought as he leaned back against the tree trunk and closed his eyes. Although there was a steady stream of people passing just a few feet from him on the busy road, Simon fell asleep.

"Simon, Simon," Andrew said as he shook his shoulder, "come quickly, we've found Him. Hurry!"

"Found who?" Simon asked as he opened his eyes and blinked against the late afternoon sun.

"The Messiah! We've been talking to Him. Come and see," Andrew urged.

"Where is John?" Simon asked, regaining his senses and looking around.

"He stayed with the Messiah," Andrew excitedly replied.

"What makes you think that baptizing people makes John The Messiah?" Simon grumbled.

"John the Baptist isn't the Messiah! We saw him *baptize* The Messiah! His name is Jesus! Hurry, He's waiting!" Andrew insisted.

"Why would the Messiah need to be baptized?" Simon mumbled under his breath as he stood. "Very well, I'll go meet this fellow so we can get John, then we must be on our way. You've probably already cost us an extra day."

They went to a small room atop one of the houses in a settlement near the river. As they entered, Simon saw John sitting in front of a man who was nearly as tall as Simon. His hands were not the soft hands of a rabbi, but rough from years of labor and he certainly didn't look different from any other man. His beard was not very long and his hair fell past his shoulders. He wore a plain tunic and sandals. So this was what these boys thought The Messiah would look like!

But when Simon looked into His eyes, he saw something that did set this man apart from any other. There is a steeliness that indicates a definite purpose in the eyes, yet there is also the tenderness of a new mother. *He has a penetrating gaze – almost like this man knows what I am thinking. His voice is soft.* He rose and greeted Simon. The four of them sat down.

"You are Simon, the son of John," Jesus said. "You shall be called Cephas (which is translated Peter)." Simon was puzzled by this. *How did He know my name? Had the boys told Him? Why would this man call me "a stone?"*

"My brother claims that you are the Messiah," challenged Simon. "Is that the truth?"

"Are you seeking the Messiah?" Jesus asked.

"All men seek Him," Simon parried.

"What are you looking for – another King David?"

"The Scripture tells us that the Messiah will set His people free."

"There are many kinds of freedom."

"You speak in riddles," Simon said impatiently as he rose to leave. "We must be going."

Andrew and John had been silently watching the exchange, but they weren't ready to go.

"We have many more questions, Simon," John protested.

"You can stay, but Andrew and I must be going. There are fish to be caught and I have a family to feed," Simon snapped as he reached the doorway.

All the way back to Galilee, Andrew and John talked about Jesus. *He really captivated them. I wonder what the man is really after. He definitely has a purpose, but He didn't reveal a thing in our short conversation. And His eyes. Never have I seen such eyes. It is as if He could look right into my soul.*

Although he tried to ignore their conversation, Simon found himself listening as the young men discussed the strange things the Man had said and by the afternoon of the next day he discovered that he wasn't resisting the idea that this Man might be the Promised One of Israel.

Rebecca met Simon at the door when he arrived at home. "Did you see Aaron and Jude as you came?" she asked referring to Simon's younger brothers who had remained to work on the boat in his absence.

"Yes, they are on the way home," he answered as he sat on the stool by the door.

"Good! I missed you. Why were you delayed?" she asked as she took his cloak, hung it on a peg and knelt to wash his feet.

"That feels good," Simon said leaning back against the wall. "Andrew and John 'found' the Messiah."

"What are you saying?"

"On the way back, as we were crossing the Jordan River, they saw that man, John the Baptizer, in a group of people and wanted to go see what he was doing, so I rested a bit while they went. Then Andrew came back and told me they had found the Messiah. He wanted me to come meet Him. John had stayed with Him and we had to get him, so I went."

"Do you think the baptizer is the Messiah?" she asked.

"No," he answered, "and he was not who they were talking about, either. They had found another Man, named Jesus. The boys said that when this Man was baptized, a dove came down and rested on Him. They talked about Him all the way home. After three days of hearing about the things He told them, I think I could almost believe in Him myself."

That was the beginning, but I wasn't yet convinced, Peter remembered. *Still, even though I tried to put it out of my mind, I thought a lot about all that the boys said on the way home. But I had a family to care for, so I concentrated on that and went about my daily life.*

Spring turned to summer and the days rolled on in their normal way. It felt good to be fishing again. Even the familiar task of cleaning and mending the nets seemed to be more agreeable these days, but Simon was always glad for the Sabbath and the rest it meant. As was his custom, he and his brothers went to synagogue to worship on that particular Sabbath. Nearing the building, Andrew stopped and grabbed Simon's arm.

"Look, there is Jesus," he said as he pointed Him out.
"It is," agreed Simon.
"Let's go talk to Him," Andrew urged.
"Go ahead," Simon answered, "the rest of us will go on in." Andrew quickly found John and together they approached Jesus.

About the time services began, Andrew and John slipped into their seats. The priest indicated where Jesus was to be seated on the bema, the place where the Scripture was read and the teaching occurred. At the proper time, Jesus was handed the scroll. He opened and read from it, then taught. He did not shout as some did when they read the Scripture and taught. His voice seemed to caress the listeners' ears, but it was clear and resonant enough to be heard by everyone. Suddenly a man arose from his seat and began shouting and cursing, saying,

"Let us alone! What have you to do with us, Jesus of Nazareth? Have you come to destroy us? I know who you are – the Holy One of God."

"Be silent, and come out of him!" Jesus said in a calm, authoritative voice. Suddenly it was as if the man was thrown down in the middle of the floor by someone unseen. He convulsed several times, then grew quiet. A few men went to him. The man lay very still for a while. His eyes blinked rapidly and tears started forming in his eyes. His hand reached toward Jesus, who was standing near him.

Kneeling, Jesus took his hand in both of His and spoke softly to him. Then the man sat up. Jesus continued talking softly, privately, to him. Finally, he arose and returned to his seat with his head bowed. Jesus resumed speaking to the amazed crowd as if nothing unusual had occurred.

At the end of the teaching, John and Andrew told

Simon about the invitation they had given to Jesus to join them for the Sabbath meal.

"Good," Simon answered, "now I'll see what He is really about."

"Blessed Sabbath, Peter," Jesus said as He joined the small group.

When they reached Simon's house, Rebecca met them at the door.

"Andrew invited Jesus to eat with us today. He's the Man they found at the Jordan River." Simon told her. "Now we can see what He is all about," he whispered.

"I am glad that You do us the honor of sharing a meal with us this day," Rebecca smilingly welcomed. "Please excuse my mother. She is ill with a fever or she would join us."

"May I meet your mother?" Jesus inquired.

Rebecca looked at Him closely, then nodded and took Him to the room where her mother lay on a bed. Simon watched from the doorway. The sick woman looked up at Jesus as He laid His hand on her brow. Looking up to the heavens, He said a simple prayer. A look of amazement came over the face of Simon's mother-in-law, her eyes suddenly bright with joy.

"My fever is gone!" she exclaimed. Rebecca reached out, felt her mother's head, then her own and turned to Simon.

"Her head is as cool as mine," she said incredulously.

The older woman slowly arose, bowed her head to Jesus in appreciation and went out of the room to finish preparing the meal, which she, her daughter and granddaughter then served to Jesus, Simon, Andrew, John, Aaron, Jude and Eli. Little Deborah sat at her father's feet.

"I have never heard teaching like yours," stated Simon,

"nor seen anything like that which occurred today. What really happened in the synagogue?" The younger boys leaned forward in rapt attention.

"The man you witnessed in the synagogue had a demon," Jesus answered. "I cast it out of him and he was restored."

"And then You came here and healed my mother-in-law," Simon said. "What is the source of Your power? Are You a prophet, gifted by God?"

"My power is indeed from God," Jesus affirmed.

"Is God the source of the wisdom of Your teachings, too?" Andrew asked.

"God is the source of everything I am or have," Jesus answered.

"You speak so casually about casting out demons," Simon observed, but before he finished his question, there was a loud pounding on the door of Simon's house.

"Where is He? We have brought a sick man for Him to heal. Jesus smiled at His hosts and excused Himself, saying that He must be about His Father's business as He headed for the door. When He opened it, He was greeted with a shout and waded into a crowd. Simon, Andrew and John watched from the doorway of the house. There in the street, Jesus laid hands on those who had been brought to Him and answered the needs of the gathering throng until evening fell. When the people returned to their homes, Jesus left Capernaum and headed in the direction of his home town, Nazareth.

It had been nearly two weeks since Jesus had dined with them and Simon couldn't stop thinking about the many miracles he had seen this Man perform that Sabbath. *Truly, there is something very special about this Rabbi. What He teaches is unlike anything I have ever heard before and the authority with which He moves and speaks is even greater than I have seen in the priests and rabbis in the Temple at Jerusalem. And then there are the healings and other miracles.* Simon knew that this Man was unique, but *is He truly sent from God?*

Wiping the sweat from his brow, Simon looked around the boat, he was checking in preparation for this evening's fishing. It appeared to be in good shape so he checked the gear aboard, the ropes and sails, the container of oil and lamps. He called Andrew, who was completing a check of the nets for tears, and they went home for the midday meal and to rest until nearly sunset. When the sun began its slow slide to the horizon, they would sup with the family, then set out for another night of fishing with their partners on Zebedee's boat.

Simon's crew consisted of his three younger brothers but Zebedee had only two sons and a slightly larger vessel, so he had two hired men to complete his crew. The two owners had found that if they fished together, both were more successful and if one boat had a problem, help was near at hand.

They put out about sunset. By the time they arrived at their selected area, night had closed in around them. Simon loved the cool breeze on his face. All around on the water he saw the oil lamps of other boats flickering like fireflies in the summer evening. The moon high above them illuminated the water making it a silvery carpet. *There is no other work a man can do that is as pleasing to the soul as fishing,* he thought.

The two boats were about thirty cubits apart. Simon and Andrew went to the bow and deftly cast a net from each side of the vessel. Nets were cast on both sides of Zebedee's boat, too. After allowing time for the nets to sink to the desired depth, Aaron and Jude, helped haul them back into Simon's boat. Even before the nets surfaced, the experienced fishermen knew how much the cast had netted by how hard they had to pull.

The catch this night was like the others they had brought in this week – nothing to take home. The ones they did catch were so small the men were surprised that they had even stayed in the net. After several more fruitless attempts, they took a break to eat some dates and bread.

"The breeze is coming up." Andrew observed.

"Yes," Simon replied, "we'd better head in."

They signaled their decision to Zebedee's boat and the men started setting the sails so that the winds would lend them a hand. The wind picked up quickly and soon waves were washing over the sides of the boats. When the wind suddenly turned, the crews scurried to take the sails down. Manning the oars, they strained against the now roaring sea.

Finally they struck land. Two men jumped out of the boat and started dragging it farther up on the sand. The others joined them and soon they had the boat safely beached. Simon looked down the strand and saw that Zebedee's boat had also made it back safely. The drenched men headed for the warmth of their homes. There would be no fish this night.

Because the catch had been minimal for weeks now, the men had found it necessary to work until the sun rose well above the hills. Although the take was sparse again this morning, Simon had decided that today they would head home shortly after the sun rose and accordingly signaled the other boat. Suddenly, John hollered over from his father's boat. He was pointing toward a place on the other side of Zebedee's boat.

"Andrew, look over there! It's Him!"

"Simon," Andrew said to his brother, "let's put in over there and see what John is yelling about."

"We might as well," Simon answered. "We've already spent the whole of the night."

With that, both boats turned toward the place where a crowd was beginning to form along the shore. It was growing by the minute and spreading up the gentle green slope. Men, women and children kept coming and at the center of it was Jesus. By the time the vessels had landed, the crowd nearly reached to the top of the hill.

Jesus was seated on a large stone near the lake and the crowd sat on the grass to listen to what He had to say. Simon set about tending to his usual duties after fishing, but they had beached near enough to where Jesus was standing that he could hear the Man's voice addressing the growing crowd. He was impressed again with what he heard as Jesus began to talk. His voice was clear and vibrant, carrying to the entire assembly. The people listened attentively. Almost unconsciously, the crowd inched closer to Him, as if they didn't want to miss a single word. When he finished cleaning the nets and replaced them in the boat, Simon sat down to listen.

Looking around, Jesus saw the two boats beached nearby and Simon sitting next to the smaller vessel. Jesus walked over to the boat.

"Peter, could you put out just a bit?" Jesus called to him. Simon nodded and Jesus climbed over the side and seated Himself in the center of the vessel. Simon heaved the bow so that it skidded off the beach into the water. He jumped on board and, with the oars, kept it close to the land near the crowd. Jesus moved to the bow, sat down and continued teaching. After a while, He stopped talking and turned.

"Put out into the deep and let down your nets for a

catch," Jesus told Simon.

"Master, we toiled all night and took nothing! But at your word I will let down the nets," Simon answered. Signaling to his brothers, who swam out and clamored over the sides of the little vessel, they put out and cast the nets as Jesus had instructed.

When they began to pull the nets up, they realized how big the catch was going to be and signaled their partners in the other boat, who immediately cast off and joined them. They put the fish into the two boats. The catch was so great that both boats settled down until the water was nearly spilling into them. They rowed the short distance to land. As soon as they were on the beach, Simon fell at Jesus' feet.

"Depart from me, for I am a sinful man, O Lord," he cried.

"Do not be afraid, Peter," Jesus told him, "from now on you will be catching men. Come, follow Me."

Simon turned to Zebedee and told him, "You are in charge. I must follow this man." And to his brothers, he said,

"Do all Zebedee tells you. He is now in charge." He turned and ran to catch up to the rabbi.

"I'm going, too," called Andrew as he hurried after Jesus and Simon, who would be known from this time forward as Peter, the name Jesus gave him.

That was the beginning of the three most extraordinary years of Peter's life. His brothers had continued the fishing business, fulfilling the needs of his family and Peter was never sorry that he had chosen to follow Jesus that day. At least not until the night he had so miserably failed Him. These memories haunted him now.

Jesus had told him as they walked out of the city and across the Kidron Valley to the Garden of Gethsemane that fateful night,

"Simon, Simon, behold, Satan demanded to have you, that he might sift you like wheat, but I have prayed for you that your faith may not fail. And when you have turned again, strengthen your brothers." Peter protested,

"Lord, I am ready to go with You to prison and to death." That had all been bravado, he realized now as he hung his head remembering Jesus' prediction, "I tell you, Peter, the cock will not crow this day before you will deny three times that you know Me."

I had been so certain of my commitment to Jesus that I tried to protect Him with my fisherman's knife. In the melee, I cut off the ear of one of the High Priest's servants who was with them. Jesus' eyes admonished me as He picked up the ear and replaced it, healing it completely. While the temple guards arrested Him, John and I melted into the crowd and followed them back into the city. Finally we found ourselves at the house of the High Priest. The soldiers told everyone in the crowd to wait in the courtyard. The high priest would need witnesses to the events of the night. As we crouched around fires which had been lit to ward off the night chill, a young servant girl approached me, intently staring.

"This man was also with Him," she announced loudly.

"Woman, I do not know Him," Peter retorted just as loudly. Those standing around the fire looked at both of them and each other, but soon their attention returned to the fire. The people in the courtyard milled around. Some of them knew each other, but most did not, so the conversation was sparse.

Then it happened again! A man wearing tattered clothing stood next to Peter, and when his gaze fell on Peter's face, his eyes lit with recognition.

"You are also one of them," he said loudly.

"Man, I am not!" Peter stated emphatically, as his heart raced. That seemed to satisfy those who had heard the accusation and the people continued as before.

About an hour passed and the crowd's attention was drawn to the steps of Caiaphas' house, where the guard was transferring Jesus to the dungeon where he would be held until dawn. Suddenly one of the men standing near Peter began pointing to him.

"Certainly this man also was with Him, for he, too, is also a Galilean," he confidently stated. Peter's heart drummed against his chest. He feared that they would arrest and try him, too.

"Man, I do not know what you are talking about," Peter answered. The cock crowed as he made this avowal. He looked up and saw Jesus looking at him. The Master had predicted this very thing earlier this night and he had denied its validity. Tears streamed from his eyes as he turned and dashed from the courtyard. John followed him, but when he found Peter inconsolable, he returned to the courtyard. Peter stumbled through the dark streets, blinded by tears of remorse.

I considered myself to be the strongest of the disciples, always ready to defend the Master and bold in my fervent desire to serve Him. But tonight I proved to be the weakest of them all! Even young John shows more dedication to the Lord than I do!

Eventually, Peter reached the quarters he and several of the disciples had rented for the celebration. No one was there now. He remained in the main room alone, slumped in a corner, his face buried in his hands and his clothing soaked by his tears. *I am such a failure! I refused to admit to myself that I am a coward at heart —I have failed other times, too — like the time I tried to show how genuine my faith was by walking on water as the Lord was doing.*

Jesus had been teaching on the side of the Sea of Galilee opposite Capernaum. When He finished His teaching He had told the disciples to take the boat and return home. When they left, Jesus dismissed the crowd and went alone up on a hill to pray. Evening came and Jesus looked up from his prayers and gazed out on the lake. There He saw the disciples struggling to row the boat, which was caught in a violent storm, such as is common to that part of the Sea of Galilee.

Arising from His prayers, Jesus walked down to the shore and across the churning water toward the boat. One of the men saw Him coming and shouted above the storm that Jesus' ghost was coming toward them. Everyone cried out in fear,

"It is a ghost!" Then they heard Jesus' calm voice saying,

"Take heart; it is I. Do not be afraid." Those words quieted them somewhat, but Peter still couldn't quite believe his eyes. He felt a need to test his faith and prove his leadership.

"Lord, if it is You, command me to come to You on the water," challenged Peter in a show of bravery.

"Come," Jesus said, holding out His hand in invitation. Cautiously, Peter began to climb out of the safety of the boat. He placed one foot on the water. He looked Jesus in the eyes and held His gaze as he lifted his other leg over the side and placed it on the waves. When he was fully free of the vessel, he took a tentative step toward his Master, never breaking eye contact. Then another step. Then another one.

He was amazed at his progress and looked down in disbelief at the angry sea about him. Suddenly he began to sink. Fear gripped him and in panic he cried out,

"Lord save me."

Immediately Jesus stretched out His hand and taking

hold of Peter's hand caught him, saying,
"O you of little faith, why did you doubt?"

It was true – I had doubted Jesus. I knew that He was the power, but when I looked at the waves, I lost my focus on Him. Now I have betrayed Him in my fear this final time. How could I, the leader, have allowed fear to make me do such a thing? It seems like all too frequently I tried to step out in leadership of the band of disciples and was chastened by the Master. Yet Jesus encouraged me to lead the others. Maybe I go too far. Like on the day we were walking to Caesarea Phillippi.

Jesus was explaining to the disciples a number of things that were on His mind. Suddenly stopping, Jesus turned to the band and asked,
"Who do people say that I am?"
"Some say John the Baptist," answered Andrew.
"Elijah," added James.
"One of the prophets," stated Matthew.
"But," Jesus interrupted, "who do you say that I am?"
Without hesitation, Peter had shouted, "You are the Christ." Jesus smiled broadly, this was the truth He had been teaching them for more than two years. Turning to the others, Jesus told them,
"Do not tell anyone else what you have seen here this day, or that I am the Christ. That revelation must come from My Father." Jesus continued telling them of the events coming in a short time – that He must go to Jerusalem and suffer many things from the elders, chief priests and the scribes. He said that He would be killed. *None of us understood what He was saying – He was the Christ, the Messiah who would deliver His people, so we put these things out of our minds.*

Then Peter took Jesus aside and admonished Him.

"Far be it from you, Lord! This shall never happen to you," Peter said.

Suddenly, Jesus pulled away from him and said in a commanding voice,

"Get behind Me, Satan! For you are not setting your mind on the things of God, but on the things of man." This stunned and puzzled Peter. He turned around and came back to the others. Then Jesus addressed all of them, saying,

"If anyone would come after me, let him deny himself and take up his cross and follow me. For whoever would save his life will lose it, but whoever loses his life for my sake will find it. For what will it profit a man if he gains the whole world and forfeits his soul? Or what shall a man give in return for his soul?

"For the Son of Man is going to come with his angels in the glory of his Father, and then he will repay each person according to what he has done. Truly, I say to you, there are some standing here who will not taste death until they see the Son of Man coming in his kingdom."

How can even the Master, Who has the power to forgive me, do so? What is to become of the band of disciples now that The Messiah is dead? Will the Sanhedrin try to find us now? I hate that I am afraid. This is the hardest thing I have ever faced, but I must admit that I am very afraid. And my fear has cost me everything! Even the One who offered me hope! I am even afraid to go to Golgotha when they put Him to death!

Peter buried his head more deeply in his hands and wept the inconsolable, bitter tears of regret and despair.

John, the Beloved

John 15:9-10
As the Father has loved me, so have I loved you. Abide in my love. If you keep my commandments, you will abide in my love, just as I have kept my Father's commandments and abide in his love.

When John and his mother, Salome, brought Jesus' mother, Mary, from the foot of the cross to John's quarters while in Jerusalem, they tried to comfort her, but Mary was disconsolate. She collapsed into sobbing as soon as they reached the two rooms. Salome led her to the bed in the room she had occupied and helped her to lie down before rejoining her son in the main room. When it appeared that Mary was finally sleeping, Salome gathered her belongings and left to join the other women in the quarters they were sharing.

All the next day, Mary stayed in the room, sometimes lying down and sometimes just sitting in the lone chair, staring blankly and quietly sobbing.

That was just like Jesus – always caring about others and forgetting about Himself. I will care for Mary as I would my own mother. He knew that I was capable of such an important assignment when He saw me standing there, sharing His mother's agony. I was the only disciple in that crowd. I don't know where the others are. I haven't seen any of them except Peter since Jesus' arrest. They were probably too afraid to come. I am afraid, too, but I couldn't abandon Jesus' mother and the other faithful women who dared to be present for that awful final event. I was there to protect them if necessary. I have no weapon, but at least I was there to comfort them.

Now the reality of the loss they had suffered yesterday was sinking into his mind and he wept. Three years had passed since he left his father's boat and outraced his older, bigger brother, James, to catch up with Jesus, Peter and Andrew – that day Jesus had said, "Follow me and I will make you fishers of men." I really didn't know what Jesus meant at that time, but something inside told me that this was what I was meant to be doing.

"Where are you going?" his father, Zebedee, had called after them.

"To follow The Messiah!" he called back.

"You're too young to do that," he heard Zebedee yell, but neither of the brothers had ever looked back. And not once had he regretted his choice. But now it appeared that all was lost. He hadn't gone to synagogue this Sabbath day. Those who followed Jesus in Jerusalem were afraid to show their faces at any religious place for fear that they, too, might be arrested and put to death.

Strange, he thought, *this is the first time I feel like a mature man. I am the youngest of both the disciples and my father's family. My father still thinks of me as a boy, incapable of thinking on my own. "When you grow up," his statements to me always begin. "When you grow up," that thought upsets me more every time I hear it. I am a grown man now. I am the one the family entrusted with their very livelihood for, not only did I work like all the others on my father's boat catching the fish, but when those fish were cured, I was the one who made the long, dangerous trip through Samaria to Jerusalem to deliver the fish to the wealthy families. That was a big responsibility! None of the other men made the journey! I liked this duty. I got to know the people who live in Jerusalem – even some of the servants in the household of the high priest.*

They never treated me as though I was too young. And, although Jesus always treated me like a son – to be taught and nurtured and admonished when necessary, He also treated me like a man. Now He has told me to take care of His own mother – the woman who had carried the Messiah in her womb! There is nothing more meaningful I could ever do!

John didn't know how much time had passed when he became aware that Mary was again awake, sobbing and talking. He strained to listen to hear her words.

"My Son, my Son," she cried between wracking sobs. "I did not fully understand until now the prediction of the old man at the Temple when we consecrated You at my purification. He told me that a sword would pierce my own soul. The same spear that pierced Your dear body will be a constant wound to my soul, too. I don't understand why You had to be taken away so soon, but I know that our heavenly Father knows best – that He only lent You to me for a time. You were His gift to me and to the world. I was so sure that Your work would last for many years. Still, I am grateful for the time that we had with You. I prayed that Your brothers and sisters would accept that You were ours only for a time – that You always belonged and will forever belong to the Lord Almighty – that You were always, first and foremost, His Son – our Savior. I pray that someday they will understand. Oh, my God! Be with me in my grief. Teach me to live in my Son's memory and to Your glory as He did."

When he entered the room, John saw Mary kneeling beside the bed, her face buried in her arms, crying softly. Kneeling next her, John put his arms around her shoulders and drew her head to his chest. She had cried out words that were in his heart, too. This day was so very different from the day Jesus had taken him, James and Peter up on the high mountain. What a glorious day that had been!

Early that morning, Jesus and the disciples left the city of Caesarea Philippi and were walking toward a high mountain. At midday they stopped in a shady place by the headwaters of the Jordan River to eat and rest. Jesus looked at His followers. Most of them were sitting on stones or leaning against trees. Their conversation was easy. They were an unlikely lot, but He loved them. And they had grown to love Him.

Jesus told the group that they should stay here and wait while He took Peter, James and John farther up the mountain. This was not unusual. Jesus frequently took several aside for a more intense discussion of some point He wanted to clarify.

It was a long climb – hours long – John remembered, *but when we reached the stopping place, it was worth every step. I turned around and the whole world stretched out before me. I could even see the Sea of Galilee, though it looked small from so great a distance. Then a cloud formed and obscured the wonderful panorama. A shudder ran through my body and when I turned toward Jesus and the others I was astonished at what I saw.*

Jesus looked completely different! His garments were so dazzling white that they shone with brilliance. His face was serene, yet it radiated like the sun. He looked at ease. Like He was where He belonged. There were two other figures talking with Him and suddenly, without explanation, I knew who they were – the prophet Moses and the prophet Elijah. They, too, were clothed in radiance.

I heard Peter saying something about building three tabernacles, but I was so amazed by the scene, that all I could do was look as in a trance. Suddenly, a mighty voice came from the cloud saying, "This is My Beloved Son, with Whom I am well pleased. Listen to Him!"

All three of us fell to the ground on our faces. I couldn't stop shaking with awe. I wasn't sure of what I had seen, but it changed me. From that time I knew, without a single doubt, that Jesus was the One I would follow all of my life.

"Arise," Jesus said as he touched John's shoulder, "do not be afraid."

Looking up, John saw only Jesus standing there smiling at him. "Master," he started to say, but Jesus touched His finger to his lips, saying,

"Tell no one the vision, until the Son of Man is raised from the dead." John remembered this saying now and marveled that he had not thought about it before. *Jesus said that He would rise from the dead!*

Now, in this lonely room, with Jesus' mother in his arms, John turned these thoughts and more over and over in his mind. He thought about the conversation the little group had as they descended the mountain.

They had accepted Jesus' instruction without question, but when the subject of the coming of the Messiah arose, James asked, "Then why do the scribes say that first Elijah must come?"

"Elijah does come, and he will restore all things," answered Jesus, "but I tell you that Elijah has already come, and they did not recognize him, but did to him whatever they pleased. So also the Son of Man will certainly suffer at their hands."

That was when we realized that John the Baptist was the "Elijah" of which He spoke!

Mary's tears had subsided now. John gently lifted her to her feet and helped her to sit on the narrow bed in the corner of the room. He offered to get some food for her, but she declined.

"Lie down for a bit, Mother," he told her, "the day is now drawing to a close and we all need some rest." Mary nodded and lay down. John walked into the other room and gazed out the window at the deepening shadows.

There was a knock at the door. When John opened it, he saw Peter, but it was not the same Peter he had known all his life. This man had the look of total despair. John stepped aside. Peter entered and strode to the lone stool in the room. Sitting down heavily, he put his head in his hands and wept. Neither of them spoke a word. John stood beside Peter with his hand on his shoulder for a few minutes, then went back to the window and his own thoughts.

His mind raced as he began to remember some of the things Jesus had told His friends, as He had called them during their last supper together.

He warned us of the things which have now happened, but He left us with a word of hope. Jesus told us, "Truly, truly, I say to you, you will weep and lament, but the world will rejoice. You will be sorrowful, but your sorrow will turn into joy." That didn't mean anything to me then, but now, I wonder exactly what it does mean. What could possibly happen that could turn this great sorrow into joy? How would it come to pass? Could Jesus really do something miraculous, like rising from the dead, to bring forth His kingdom? If so, when?

As John pondered these things, Peter got up and left the room without speaking a word. John watched him walking out the door as if in a dream, not conscious of where he was going, lost. *I don't have anything to say that would help him,* John thought as the door closed. *I don't even have anything to say to help myself.*

He gazed out the window into the sparkling heavens. He knew that the sound of Peter's retreating footsteps on the stones of the street echoed the hollowness Peter was feeling inside, but John now remembered something that made his heart leap with joy! *Jesus told us that He would come again. He has always kept His promises. We will see Him again. I know it! He is the Christ!*

Andrew, the Gatherer

John 6:37
***All that the Father gives me will come to me, and
whoever comes to me I will never cast out.***

With the setting sun, Andrew knew the Sabbath had ended. He didn't move, but just lay still on the roof of the house of Mary, Martha and Lazarus in Bethany where the little band had fled from the Garden of Gethsemane night before last. He tried to blink away the tears that continually welled up in his eyes and tried to see the stars as they appeared. These had been the longest two days of his life, both in time span and in lost hopes for the future.

Jesus is the Messiah, I am sure of that! But the traveler who came from Jerusalem late yesterday afternoon brought the distressing news that Jesus had been crucified between two thieves. I couldn't believe that it was true! How can the Son of God be dead? But the messenger was telling the truth and I knew it!

There was so much confusion that night. It all began with what Jesus said while we were at table when He told us that one of us would betray Him. None of us knew who the traitor was and when Judas left, I thought that he had been assigned some special mission. Not until I saw him at the head of the company of torch-bearing temple guards who passed us in the garden did I have an inkling that Judas was the one.

Jesus had known! Fear shot through all of us when we saw the guards. Immediately, we left the campfire and hid in the shadows. Soon the procession returned back down the same path. Jesus was surrounded by soldiers and the captain of the guard led them. We watched the torches passing through the trees and crept from our cover. Soon Simon, who had left us when he first saw the guards, returned with James. They told us we ought to leave the area – the guards might come after us, too. So we started winding our way through the gnarled olive trees that grow on the side of the Mount of Olives. James had been with Jesus. He told us that Peter and John had joined in with the crowd following the guards and were probably in the city. Quickly and quietly, we crossed the top of the mountain and headed for the safety of Bethany.

All of us stayed out of sight in this rooftop room of Lazarus' home. The next morning, we tried to figure out what we should do, but by afternoon we had still not come to agreement on any plan. We realized that no one was looking for us, yet we were reluctant to return to Jerusalem to seek the others. Then, toward evening, the traveler arrived from Jerusalem and we learned of Jesus' death. Peter and John had not yet joined us. By then it was Sabbath and the city gates would be closed, so we were not able to look for them until Sabbath ended. We didn't go to the synagogue today with our hosts. Instead we brooded over the dismal events that had occurred.

Finally, Andrew's thoughts turned to happier times – times of laughter and humor. He remembered the day not long ago when he had seen a group of children playing near where Jesus was teaching. There were fifteen or twenty small children and four older girls who seemed to be watching the younger ones. He walked up to one of them.

"Their parents are listening to the teacher," she explained.

"It is kind of you to watch over these small ones," Andrew answered. "Do you know who the teacher is?

"He is a rabbi," offered a black-haired, bright-eyed tot standing by the girl. "That is true," Andrew agreed and turning to the older girl, he added. "He is the Messiah."

"How can that be?" the girl asked. "He is no different from any of us."

"That may appear to be true," Andrew replied, "but He is the Messiah. Would the children like to meet Him?"

"Oh, yes!" replied the little one.

"Now, Miriam," the older girl chided, "why would such small ones as you are be allowed to meet the Messiah?"

"Because He loves us," she answered. The older girl shrugged her shoulders. Andrew smiled as he reached down and took the child's hand.

"Come," he invited, "You'll see."

The older girls took the hands of smaller ones and the entire group followed Andrew. The children's mothers, seeing what was occurring, joined the bunch, taking the hands of their children in case they were turned away. Some of the disciples who were sitting near Jesus arose and began to try to divert the tiny procession, but Jesus spoke.

"Let the children come to me; do not hinder them." He smiled broadly and held out His arms in welcome.

"See," Andrew smiled at the older girl as they approached. Andrew looked down at Miriam and winked. The child beamed an "I told you so" at the older girl.

When they reached Jesus, He picked her up and sat her on his lap. Miriam looked up into His smiling face and laid her head against His chest as He continued addressing the crowd.

"For to such belongs the kingdom of God. Truly, I say to you, whoever does not receive the kingdom of God like a child shall not enter it." Jesus placed His hand on Miriam's shoulder and blessed her. When she wiggled off His lap, the other children came and lovingly He blessed each one. The disciples stood nearby in awe of the Master's apparent enjoyment of the interruption. After receiving their blessings, the children scampered off like frisky lambs and the mothers and older girls who were waiting for them scurried to keep up and regain control of their charges.

Later that night, Jesus approached Andrew.

"You did well to bring the children to Me today," He said. "That is what My teaching is all about. When you bring others to Me, I will never turn them away."

Andrew was always bringing someone to meet Jesus and was never rebuked, for that kind of interruption was always welcome. Sometimes, he had found just the right person in the crowds that followed them.

One day Jesus had taught in the morning, then He and the disciples crossed the Sea of Galilee so they could have a private conversation, but when the people saw where they were going they walked around the upper end of the lake to where the boat landed.

Jesus and the disciples went up on a mountain and sat down. When He looked up, He saw a large crowd of people, about five thousand men and their families, coming to them. Jesus, full of pity for them as the place was deserted and they had traveled far to reach Him, turned to Philip.

"Where are we to buy bread, so that these people may eat?" He asked.

"Master," said Philip. "Two hundred denarii worth of bread would not be enough for each of them to get a little."

"There is a boy here who has five barley loaves and two fish, but what are they for so many?" Andrew said as he drew nearer the small boy who was with him.

"They are yours," the boy said, offering them to Jesus. The disciples began scoffing about how little it was for so large a crowd. Jesus looked at them and they stopped.

"Have the people sit down," He told them and the disciples carried out the instruction. Thanking the lad for his offering, Jesus asked for some baskets to be brought and took the five loaves and the two small fish in His hands and looked up to heaven. He blessed the food and placed it in one of the baskets. Then He told the disciples to divide it into the other baskets until they each had some. As each man received a portion, more appeared and they distributed it among the seated people. When the crowd had eaten and were satisfied, Jesus told the disciples to gather up the fragments that remained, so nothing would be lost. *We collected twelve baskets full! We were amazed for we knew how little had been offered. So was the crowd, for they said, "This is indeed the Prophet who is to come into the world!"*

Andrew also remembered the way Jesus had joined in the easy camaraderie the disciples shared as they walked along from place to place. He was quick with a laugh when someone made a play on words or when one pulled a prank on another.

One day the group was walking along the road, casually plucking a few heads from the wheat left growing alongside the road when the field was harvested. This was the custom as a way to help travelers and the poor who gleaned it for their sustenance. They rolled the heads between their palms, then blew the chaff away and ate the remaining grain a few kernels at a time.

"Andrew," John began, "I've seen you bring people to meet Jesus many times. Why do you do that?"

"Because," he answered, "I still remember how I felt

the first time I met Jesus – it changed something in me and I want other people to know that wonderful feeling."

"But why did you bring the children the other day?"

Without hesitation, Andrew answered, "They needed to know Him, too."

"Oh, they were more interested in playing," John parried.

"Did you see the looks on heir faces when the Master spoke directly to them? And when He touched them? Andrew asked. Turning, he saw the smirk on John's face. Reaching down for another handful of grain, John continued,

"Have you noticed that whenever you bring someone to meet the Master, He immediately uses the situation to teach a lesson? I loved how He told the crowd that we must be like little children to enter the kingdom of heaven, but what do you think He meant by that?"

Andrew thought for a minute, popping some kernels of grain into his mouth and chewing thoughtfully before he answered.

"A little child hasn't formed his thoughts completely," he said slowly, weighing his words carefully so that he could say what he was thinking. "He is still open-minded and ready to receive. He allows his mind to play with the things which are presented to him and when he grasps a thought completely, it is his forever. That is how we should all be."

"That is insight from heaven," said Jesus, who had overheard the conversation. "You have received it as a little child, Andrew. Keep bringing people to Me as that is the task for which you are commissioned."

"Master, why do you encourage him to continually interrupt Your teaching?" asked John with a grin.

"All things that happen the Father uses to teach us

something about life -- even when you joke with one another," Jesus said and playfully pushed John's shoulder with a laugh. Andrew loved the way Jesus joined their fun. Sometimes, even when He taught, He told humorous stories. A couple of days earlier Andrew had turned his head to hide a smile when Jesus was addressing a crowd.

"How can you say to your brother, 'Let me take the speck out of your eye,' when there is the log in your own eye?" Jesus asked them. "You hypocrite, first take the log out of your own eye, and then you will see clearly to take the speck out of your brother's eye." The crowd of hearers had burst into laughter, but the point was made.

That is why it seemed so strange when, in the last two or three weeks, Jesus had turned more somber and talked a lot about His death. None of us wanted to hear about that and didn't even believe that it would ever happen, because He is the Messiah. We all dismissed it from our minds, but, suddenly, on the night of Passover He was arrested and the next morning crucified. Why didn't the authorities see what we saw in Him from our first encounters? Were the Pharisees so blinded by their laws, that they had missed the Messiah and actually killed Him on a cruel tree? What could any of His followers have done to stop them? Would it have done any good if we had gone to Jesus' defense instead of running away? Did we fail our Master?

Andrew rolled over onto his side and buried his face in his arm, sobbing. He lay there quite a long time but finally he knew what the Master would want them to do. He got up and went to where Simon the Zealot was laying. Shaking him awake, he told him of his thoughts and together they roused the others. It would soon be dawn and the city gates of Jerusalem would be opened. They would be there at that time and go to find John and Peter, who had gone into the city with the crowd after the arrest. Those two had stayed in the city on the Sabbath. Today they would probably be at Mary's home, their usual meeting place. That would be the first place they would check. *Perhaps a new day will bring answers to many questions and a new perspective on which we can act.*

Matthew, Tax Collector

Romans 3:21b-24
For there is no distinction: for all have sinned and fall short of the glory of God, and are justified by his grace as a gift, through the redemption that is in Christ Jesus.

Matthew wrung his hands as he paced back and forth in the tiny rooftop room he was sharing with the other eight disciples who had fled to Bethany that dreadful night of Jesus' arrest. *Everything happened so fast! I'm not even sure exactly what did happen, but I know one thing for certain – I can't go back to the life I led before I met Jesus! All of my future is built on my faith in Jesus. Nothing can ever be the same as it was.*

The lives of hundreds of other people, too, have been touched during the three years Jesus walked the dusty roads of Israel telling them about a new way to live – a way they could be free in spite of Roman oppression. Jesus tried to get us to accept that the circumstances we were living in at this particular time – or at any particular time – have very little to do with the way things turn out in our lives, but nobody seemed to get it. I'm not sure that I got it all, but I have absorbed enough to change my life for the better.

All of his life Matthew had fought an uphill battle. As

a child, Levi, as he was known then, had been different from the other boys in synagogue and tried hard to be accepted by them, but he always seemed to be the scapegoat for everything that happened. When the abuse didn't end with his schooling, he bought the job of tax gatherer for the Romans. His purpose, at least partly, was that he saw in it a way to take retribution on those who had caused him such misery in his earlier years. It didn't matter at all to him that he was the most hated man in Galilee. The Romans were satisfied with his work. He paid them more than they required and still had a good income.

Capernaum was one of the most profitable posts a publican could hold. It was on the main trade route from Persia and the Orient to Egypt and the west. The caravans didn't protest the tax he charged them, unless it became too exorbitant. In that case, the owners of the caravan might go to Rome and press a charge against him, but Levi could crowd the limit without exceeding it. He also knew how far he could push the locals – an advantage he relished and used punitively.

He had a home with two servants and oversaw ten underling tax collectors. He was very comfortable in almost every way. Still, something he couldn't name sometimes bothered him. He was able to push it out of his mind, except at night. In the quiet that was supposed to embrace sleep, he often found himself filled with unrest for which he couldn't account. Yet He was satisfied with his life – until the day he met Jesus face to face.

There He is again, Levi thought to himself as he saw the rabbi, Jesus, walk past the door of the drab tax collector's office. *I wonder what He is saying that draws such crowds? He just seems to wander around talking and people follow Him. What can He be telling them? This rabbi has come to Capernaum a number of times the past few months and each time, He draws more people than before. There are excited stories of how He is healing lame or blind people and driving out demons, but I've seen other so-called prophets do such miracles before, only to hear that the "cures" didn't last much longer than the prophet was in town. This One is probably another one of those,* he mused. *And yet, this Man has come repeatedly and the miracles are apparently permanent, so what is He all about? Maybe I should go listen to what He is telling them,* Levi decided. Turning to his clerk, he said, "I'm going to be out for a short time." Confidently, he strode toward where people were gathering a short way down the street. He stopped at the back of the crowd where he could listen unobserved.

Jesus was sitting on the edge of the village well, saying, "And when you fast, do not look gloomy like the hypocrites, for they disfigure their faces that their fasting may be seen by others." Levi smirked to himself. *He sure has them figured out,* he thought. Smugly, he smiled as he listened.

"Do not lay up for yourselves treasures on earth, where moth and rust destroy and where thieves break in and steal, but lay up for yourselves treasures in heaven, where neither moth nor rust destroys and where thieves do not break in and steal. For where your treasure is, there your heart will be also," Jesus told them. Levi shook his head.

"How do you do that?" he muttered as he turned around and went back to his office. *The Man just didn't understand the realities of life,* he thought as he kicked at a stone in his path. *It takes money to buy the things you want in life. If you don't store it up, how can you be happy? He is a dreamer,* he concluded.

By the time he reached his office, Levi was convinced that the Man was another of those teachers who came by every so often spouting foolishness of some kind. He put it out of his mind when he went out to inspect a large caravan which was passing through the area, but on the way back to his office, he found that his thoughts had once again returned to this Jesus and what He said. *How could one store up treasures in heaven? Did he mean that a person should go through life with only the bare necessities?* The questions overwhelmed him. *It was all so much drivel,* he decided and once again put it out of his mind, but somehow he felt drawn to the Man in spite of his misgivings.

His sleep that night was troubled. *That Jesus keeps invading my dreams. Why is He smiling at me? Doesn't He know who I am? None of the religious people even look at me in the street. I am hated by everyone in town and I sneer at them. They call me a sinner, because of my work for the Romans. They accept my money, but that is as far as any relationship goes. Nobody smiles at me – ever. The only "friends" I have are outcasts like me – harlots and tax collectors, but Jesus smiles at me.*

The next day, Jesus was again teaching in Capernaum and during a time when his duties were minimal, Levi left his office to go hear what He was saying. *When Jesus passed the tax office, He was headed toward the Sea of Galilee.* By the time Levi got close to the crowd, he saw that Jesus was sitting in a fishing boat and talking to those gathered on the shore.

"No one can serve two masters," Jesus said, "for either he will hate the one and love the other, or he will be devoted to the one and despise the other. You cannot serve God and money."

Levi listened carefully to learn how you could go through life without worrying about this essential thing – money.

"Look at the birds of the air," Jesus said, gesturing toward a small flock of birds flying overhead, "they neither sow nor reap nor gather into barns, and yet your heavenly Father feeds them." The flock settled in a mustard tree at the edge of the crowd. "Are you not of more value than they? And which of you by being anxious can add a single hour to his span of life?"

What is He saying, Levi wondered. *Does He mean that a man doesn't have to work? That God will provide for sluggards? How can He say such things?* Jesus pointed to the flowers blooming in profusion on the hillside and continued.

"Consider the lilies of the field, how they grow: they neither toil nor spin, yet I tell you, even Solomon in all his glory was not arrayed like one of these. But if God so clothes the grass of the field, which today is alive and tomorrow is thrown into the oven, will he not much more clothe you, O you of little faith? Therefore do not be anxious, saying, 'What shall we eat?' or 'What shall we drink?' or 'What shall we wear?' For the Gentiles seek after all these things, and your heavenly Father knows that you need them all. But seek first the kingdom of God and his righteousness, and all these things will be added to you."

Behind him, Levi heard a commotion near the tax office and hurried back to his work. As he went, more questions filled his mind. *I would like to stay and talk with Jesus, but right now, I know that I need to settle an argument.*

As he entered the small building, he saw a large, burly Ethiopian camel driver holding the arms of two of his workers. All three were shouting at the same time. With an air of authority, Levi stepped up to the trio.

"Release these men," he ordered the camel driver. The man let go of them and the two men rubbed their arms, trying to get the circulation going in them again.

"What is the problem?" Levi demanded of the camel driver.

"These men loosed all the cargo in my caravan and refused to reload my camels," he began. "Then they told me what tax I owed and it was unreasonable, so I brought them back here for you to correct it. They did not want to come, so I grabbed them and brought them."

"I see," said Levi, measuring his response, "we do not reload animals after we have examined the cargo to determine what the tax should be ..."

"You mean how much you can force us to pay," the camel driver bellowed.

"We do not determine how much the tax is, we only collect it for the Roman government," Levi replied matter-of-factly.

"Plus 'a little something' for yourself," yelled the camel driver as he grabbed Levi by both arms, lifting him into the air.

"Come now," Levi said in a still calm voice, although his heart was racing. "Put me down and tell me how much your tax amounted to. How many camels do you have in your caravan, what is the cargo and where is it to be delivered?"

With his feet back on the floor, Levi walked to the table at which he kept his records and, as he seated himself, took a clay tablet on which to work. One of the tax gatherers handed him the clay tablet he had been using to inventory the load.

The camel driver swelled with pride as he said, "I have twenty camels loaded with spices and silk from the east and I am to deliver it to the Pharaoh himself. It is a gift for the queen."

"I see," Levi said, turning toward his employees. They nodded in agreement with what the driver said. "And how much tax do they say that you owe?"

"Fifty gold shekels!"

"Well," Levi said as he studied the cargo list and wrote some figures on the tablet, "it appear that they miscalculated a bit. I see it to be forty-five gold shekels."

"That's better!" the camel driver agreed as he reached for his money pouch. He counted out the tax, glared at the two underlings, bowed to Levi and left, still muttering.

"You did well," Levi told his men, who were examining their bruised arms. He handed them each a denarius, saying,

"This will help your arms to heal faster." Levi had instructed his men to overcharge caravans loaded with luxury items bound for Egypt. He knew that most of the time, there would be no dispute on the amount and the few times it was challenged, such as today, a small adjustment would solve the problem and the caravan would be on its way. There would be enough that he could give the men a little extra to encourage them in this practice and still come out with a hefty portion left for him.

A couple of weeks later Matthew saw Jesus go down the street toward the lake again. During the intervening time, he had thought a great deal about the things he had heard the rabbi say. He looked at his own life. *I have repaid ill treatment with more of the same. I took the position of publican in order to exact retribution on those who wronged me and I have become wealthy by taking advantage of my position to legally rob both strangers who passed through this area and my own neighbors.*

My friends are other publicans, or prostitutes. No father wants a tax collector for a son-in-law, so I'm not married. I have everything that I thought I wanted, but I still feel empty. I don't even go to synagogue any more. I know that I'm not welcome there. How did I get so far adrift from the boy who wanted to be a teacher in the synagogue? My neighbors consider me a traitor. Maybe the rabbi was right. One couldn't serve two s *masters – God or riches. Maybe I chose the wrong one to follow. But is it possible for me to change now – even if I wanted to? The crowd following Jesus is much larger than it was the last time He was here,* Levi thought. *It seems that more and more people are tagging along after Him. Maybe I should go again to hear him. No, all of my men are out in the countryside gathering taxes from the locals, so I must stay here to handle any caravans today,* he concluded and settled down at the table.

It was after midday when Levi heard a footstep inside the door of the tax office and when he looked up, he was astounded to see Jesus standing before him.

"Oh, um, what can I do for you?" he stammered as he rose, knocking some clay tablets to the floor in the process.

"I have seen you several times down by the lake," answered Jesus. *His voice is so soft and musical, like a bird' song,* Levi thought.

"Follow me," Jesus said as He turned around and went out the door.

Levi was surprised when his feet started moving around the table and out the door. *What am I doing?* he thought. But by the time his feet brought him through the crowd who had been waiting in the street and alongside Jesus, his mouth took over. It said, "Please do me the honor of eating with me this evening."

"We gladly accept your invitation," Jesus answered with a smile. Then the rabbi saw a stone under a tree and sat down on it. The crowd following them gathered tightly around Him and He began to speak to them.

Levi wanted to hear what he said, but suddenly he realized that his invitation to Jesus to dine with him that evening had been accepted, so he hurried home to instruct his servants to prepare a wonderful feast for Jesus and his followers. He told them to prepare a fatted calf and a lamb and vegetables and fruits and to be sure to have plenty of fine wine for a sumptuous meal. Then he hurried back to his office, where his employees had begun to return from their daily work with reports and receipts in hand.

"Quickly," he instructed, "put the reports and collections on the table and listen to me. I want each of you to go out to my friends and invite them to sup with me tonight. I have the honor of receiving special guests I want them to meet." *My friends, too, need to know this Man.*

Without question, the workers laid their tablets and the monies they had collected on the table and left the office. Levi quickly picked up the money and took it with him to his house to put in his safe place. Then he went to the bake shop for bread and some tasty pastries. When he returned home, he told the servants how he wanted the room appointed. The table had to be at its largest so he could accommodate as many friends as possible. They just have to meet this Jesus. The couches were squeezed in as tightly as possible. Near the entrance door, two stone bowls with a goodly supply of towels and water assured that the feet of all the visitors would be washed. He had engaged additional servants on the way home. On another table near the entrance to the room were several jars of fragrant oils for anointing the heads of the visitors. Everything was arranged when he was told that the food was ready to be served. A few minutes later the first guests arrived.

When Jesus and his company of disciples approached Levi's house, a group of Pharisees who had heard about the occasion were waiting near the steps to the house to see if Jesus would dare accept the invitation. They saw the guests who had arrived earlier. One of the Pharisees caught Philip's arm as they passed and asked, "Why does He eat with tax collectors and sinners?"

Hearing the question, Jesus turned to him and replied,

"Those who are well have no need of a physician, but those who are sick. I came not to call the righteous, but sinners."

With that Jesus and the disciples ascended the steps to Levi's warm greeting and entered his house for the evening of repast and fellowship.

That night, as He was leaving Levi's house, Jesus said to him, "From this day forward, your name will be Matthew for surely you are 'a gift from God.'"

That day changed not just my name, but my life, forever. Jesus loves me – just as I am! It is as if we have been friends all of my life. He knows that I have questions, but He accepts me! I can't let go of Jesus! I see in Him the life I really want to live! I knew at the dinner that from that moment on I would forever belong with Him – to Him. I never went back to the tax office. I freed my servants, sold my house and the tax franchise to one of my friends the next day and gave all of my money to Jesus to be used for the common needs of the band. And I am much the richer for it But now what? He wondered. *What are we supposed to do now? Are we to try to continue doing the same as Jesus did? He sent us out by two's some time ago and told us to preach as He did. And yes, there were wonderful results on that mission, but can we continue to do that indefinitely without Jesus to encourage and instruct us? I still can't believe that things have happened the way they have. Jesus didn't resist His arrest at all. In earlier times, He often told us that such a thing would happen to Him, but none of us really understood how it could – until it did!*

Today total desolation filled Matthew's soul. At last the tears started to flow, rapidly increasing until there was a river from each eye. He stopped pacing and sunk down to his knees. Raising his hands to heaven he called out to God, but no sound escaped his mouth. There were no words to express his deep mourning for the One to whom he owed so much.

Simon, the Zealot

John 12:35-36
So Jesus said to them, "The light is among you for a little while longer. Walk while you have the light, lest darkness overtake you. The one who walks in the darkness does not know where he is going. While you have the light, believe in the light, that you may become sons of light."

It had all seemed so right when Judas first came up with the plan, Simon thought. *He assured me that nothing could go wrong. This was the time for action. For three years we had been following Jesus. Both of us were sure that He was the Messiah promised in the Scriptures, but He was not doing anything toward gaining Israel's freedom from Rome. Judas was so certain that his plan would force Jesus into action, leading the country to independence. I was interested at first, but something deep inside told me it was a bad idea.*

Simon had grown up in the Nationalist movement, which was strongest in Galilee. The members of this political party were devoutly committed to serving God–the one true God– who had chosen the Jews as His people. Their strong nationalistic feelings had been fanned into flame when Rome conquered Israel. Then Rome combined Israel with another captured territory to create the province of Syria – a bitter insult to Israel's pride. But the severest blow occurred when Rome called for forced allegiance to the Emperor, making him a sort of god. This action resulted in the Jewish patriots banding together and waging a guerilla war on the Romans.

Their refusal to bow down to the emperor's statue had incurred the wrath of the Roman governor. Still, the groups of Zealots were so widely dispersed throughout Galilee that Roman troops had little chance of quelling the insurgent emotions they aroused among the people. The tension had gradually mounted over the years.

When the rabbi, Jesus, came along, Simon had been drawn to hear Him to see what He was teaching that appealed to so many people. When Jesus spoke of freedom, it was music to Simon's ears, so he became more and more interested and went to hear Him frequently. One day Jesus spoke to him directly.

"Simon, I know that you love God with all your heart and are steadfast in your commitment to Him alone," Jesus said. Simon nodded his head as Jesus continued. "You have a deep longing to know the Father better and to serve Him completely." Simon could not believe his ears. This man, who knew his name although the two had never spoken before, also knew his thoughts and the yearnings of his heart!

"Yes, Rabbi, yes!" Simon enthusiastically agreed as he raised his head and looked straight into Jesus' eyes. "That is exactly what I want!" He fell to his knees and bowed to Jesus, who reached out and touched his shoulder.

"Arise, and follow me," He said, "and I will show you who God is and how to have true freedom." Eagerly, Simon rose up and became one of those who followed Him, listening to all His teaching, absorbing every word.

One night as the group prepared to go to sleep, one of the other followers, Judas Iscariot, approached him. "I believe that we have the same desire," Judas said in a low voice. "Perhaps we can help each other. We'll talk later."

Simon was puzzled by this. The man was well-spoken, obviously educated and, by his manner of speech, from Judea. *What would such a man want to do with me, a rough, uneducated, uncultured man from the Galilean hill country,* he wondered.

The opportunity to discuss anything privately didn't present itself until a few days later. Jesus had withdrawn from the band of followers to have some private time for prayer, so the rest of them were engaged in various activities. Judas walked up to Simon.

"Come with me, I want to show you something," he invited. Simon walked along beside him for a short distance before Judas stepped off the path and turned to him.

"You are one of the Zealots, aren't you?" he asked,

"Yes," Simon answered warily, "why do you ask?"

"Because my leanings are toward the nationalist party," he answered. "What do you see in this rabbi that made you want to follow Him?"

"He speaks with such authority and He talks about freedom," Simon responded. "Why do you follow Him?"

"For the same reasons," Judas replied. "He has an air of leadership about Him and wherever He goes, He draws large crowds to hear Him speak. Also, I have witnessed many signs and wonders. He casts out demons and heals the lame and blind. And I believe that Jesus is the true Messiah – the one God has sent to deliver His people from their oppression. I want to be with Him when He conquers the Roman army and drives them from our land. Isn't that what you want, too?"

"Driving the Romans out and reclaiming Israel for our God is what I dream about. I don't know if Jesus is the man who will do this thing, or not, but He intrigues me and I want to know more of Him," Simon answered.

"He is the man!" Judas proclaimed, "I know it. Wait and see! We'll talk more later," he said as he turned and they walked back to where the group was camping for the night. Parting ways, Simon went to a nearby rock, pulled his mantle around him and settled in to sleep, still wondering about the things Judas said and what he meant by them.

Nearly three years had passed and Simon was still following Jesus. He had witnessed the many miracles done during that time. He carefully listened to all that Jesus said publicly and privately to the twelve disciples He had called. He noticed that Jesus told public stories that those listening could readily relate to, but which had deeper meanings that He later explained to His circle of disciples.

Simon marveled. *Although most of what Jesus says to the masses might not be fully understood by them, the people can't seem to get enough of it. Some of His stories, even with explanation, don't answer all of my questions. Sometimes the explanation just raises more questions, but when we ask those questions, Jesus patiently answers them. Still, I have the feeling that none of us fully comprehend all that He tells us. What I really admire is the way He answers the questions from scribes and Pharisees. I wish that I was as adept as He with responses that do not fall into the snares laid for Him by adversaries.*

He remembered one Sabbath not too long ago when Jesus and the twelve had been invited to dine with a Pharisee, also named Simon. As the group was about to enter the large, impressive house, a man with dropsy approached Jesus and asked to be healed. Jesus turned to the host and other invited guests, who were watching Him closely, for they wanted to catch Him doing something unlawful thereby giving them grounds to discredit Him.

"Is it lawful to heal on the Sabbath?" Jesus asked. The men looked at one another, but no one said a word. Jesus placed His hands on the man and with a prayer to His Father, healed him. After the healed man left the area, Jesus turned again to the host and his guests.

"Which of you having a son or an ox that has fallen into a well on a Sabbath day, will not immediately pull him out?" He asked. Again He was met with silence. So Jesus and those with Him turned and continued into the house. When the guests entered the room where they were to partake of the meal, the others Simon had invited began to select their places at the table. Upon observing this, Jesus spoke.

"When you are invited by someone to a wedding feast, do not sit down in a place of honor, lest someone more distinguished than you be invited by him and he who invited you both will come and say to you, 'Give your place to this person,' and then you will begin with shame to take the lowest place. But when you are invited, go and sit in the lowest place, so that when your host comes he may say to you, 'Friend, move up higher.' Then you will be honored in the presence of all who sit at table with you. For everyone who exalts himself will be humbled, and he who humbles himself will be exalted."

Simon was amazed as Jesus continued to gently instruct those present in the manner they should give a feast. He saw that Jesus was telling them the way they should live daily life. If the guests took any offense, they all concealed it and the meal proceeded peaceably.

There is no denying Jesus' ability to lead men. He would be a good king, Simon thought and by the time Judas drew him aside again, he was ready to concede that Jesus might be the Messiah.

All of the time Simon and Judas followed Jesus they watched for a sign that He would make a move to establish His kingdom. *I grew to love and respect Jesus and would have been content to bide my time until – until forever, if that was how Jesus wanted it! But Judas couldn't let the matter go and kept attempting to draw me into his furtive plans.*

Now, in the relative safety of Bethany, Simon was wondering how everything so drastically changed in such a short time. *Only a few days ago, we were accompanied by throngs of joyful people as we made our way from Bethany to Jerusalem for the Passover observance. We had made this passage many times before, but we had never before been surrounded by multitudes singing psalms and shouting "Hosanna to the Son of David! Blessed is He who comes in the name of the Lord! Hosanna in the highest!" People laid palm branches and cloaks across the path before us. And this time, Jesus was riding the unbroken colt of a donkey, instead of walking. The crowd was jubilant, but I saw the sadness in Jesus' demeanor when He stopped the donkey at the top of the Mount of Olives, before descending into the Kidron Valley on the way to Temple Mount.*

Tears were running down Jesus' face as He looked across the valley at Jerusalem. Slowly, He said, "Would that you, even you, had known on this day the things that make for peace! But now they are hidden from your eyes. For the days will come upon you, when your enemies will set up a barricade around you and surround you and hem you in on every side and tear you down to the ground, you and your children within you. And they will not leave one stone upon another in you, because you did not know the time of your visitation." Why was He so sad? I cannot imagine that our great Jerusalem ever will be in ruins! What did He mean by visitation? What visitation? When?

It had been three evenings later, that the opportunity came and Judas again pulled Simon aside for a private talk. As they walked down a shadowy side street in Jerusalem to a quiet dead end alley, Judas again opened the subject of the coming of Jesus' kingdom. But this conversation betrayed the man's impatience. "I've been thinking about what needs to be done," he began. "I don't see Jesus doing anything toward gaining our freedom. We must do something to hurry His victory over Rome."

"Are you sure that this is something we can hurry?" Simon asked.

"Yes," Judas said reassuringly, "it is something which must be done. If we wait for Jesus to decide to claim His rightful place as Messiah and king, it may take years – years in which the Roman army will continue to brutalize our people and tax us into abject poverty. It must be done -- now! Every day that passes is a day lost."

"But when I hear Jesus talk of peace and freedom, He has such authority in His voice that I find myself thinking that perhaps He knows a better way," Simon calmly stated as they sat on a low wall at the end of the alley.

Judas was agitated. He rose and walked a short distance, stopped and returned with eyes that glittered in the moonlight. Simon backed away from him. Judas' face had a startling hardness about it, much as it had when he reproached Jesus for allowing the woman to pour costly fragrant oil over his feet the previous night.

"Why was this ointment not sold for three hundred denarii and given to the poor?" Judas had said with a snarl. To which Jesus had softly answered,

"Leave her alone, so that she may keep it for the day of my burial. For the poor you always have with you, but you do not always have me."

Judas kept the band of followers' common funds. He had smugly told Simon that when Jesus set up his kingdom, he would most likely be in charge of the treasury. Suddenly Simon caught a glimpse of Judas' real purpose in forcing the rabbi's hand – power and riches. That was what Judas really wanted – more than freedom from Roman oppression! He sought to be an important official in a new kingdom.

What was Jesus' purpose and plan? Simon wondered. *Probably not the same as that of Judas! Obviously, Jesus was in no hurry to organize and lead an army against Roman troops. But what if Jesus isn't ever going to become king? Have I wasted three years of my life following the wrong person? I'm not sure that Judas has the right answer. I am still willing to wait to see Jesus' plan.*

"I am sure that I know a way to force Jesus into action now," Judas was saying.

"Tell me what you have in mind," Simon invited. *It will do no harm to learn what Judas is thinking.*

"The Chief Priest is looking for a way to discredit Jesus so that the people will stop following Him. He is afraid the Romans will see this movement as a rebellion against Rome and blame the Jewish leaders for it. Caiaphas is sure this could unleash another wave of oppression that would make the last one look like child's play."

"How do you know this?" Simon asked.

"Shortly after we got to Jerusalem, I happened to overhear a conversation between two Sadducees and this is what they were talking about."

"It seems as if they could do this without our help."

"They are afraid of the people's reaction," answered Judas. "If they publicly arrest Him, for instance, the people may raise a protest and they don't want the Romans to think that that is the beginning of a rebellion."

"So what are you proposing?"

"If you, a Zealot who has been in Jesus' company, were to go to the Chief Priest and offer to turn Jesus over to them when he is away from the crowds, Jesus would have to defend Himself and His followers!"

"Wouldn't I be putting my neck on the block?"

"No, because they don't want the people to know about their plot. There will be no risk to you at all."

"What do you think will happen then?" Simon asked, rising to face Judas.

"If Jesus is attacked and His life is at stake, surely, if He is God's Son, God would see that this is the time to establish His kingdom in Israel and send angels to protect Jesus. They would win any battle that might ensue!" Judas assured him.

"But what if that doesn't happen? What if God doesn't send legions of angels to defend the Messiah? What if that is not God's plan?" Simon posed. "What then?"

"If that doesn't happen, and Jesus is killed, then we will know for sure that He really wasn't the Messiah," Judas said throwing up his hands and turning away. After a few steps, he turned back and in long, purposeful strides, returned to Simon. Looking him in the eyes, through clenched teeth, he stated,

"This is the time of decision – or do you want to keep wasting your time following a man who talks of freedom, but takes no action with which to secure it?"

Simon sank down onto the wall and sat there. He was baffled by this exchange. *I don't think I am afraid, for I fought fiercely against the Romans and have no fear of them, but this is different. Jesus is a man of peace and if He feels the time isn't right for Him to establish His kingdom, perhaps there is a good reason for waiting. I love Jesus and now Judas is asking me to betray the Man and His love.*

"I'm sorry, Judas," he replied, "but I can't do such a thing. I follow God and I don't believe that is what He wants me to do. Why don't you do it, if you feel so certain?"

Judas turned on him. There was a ferocious glare in his eyes. "Then I will do it. It must be done – and soon!" he growled as he stalked away.

Simon sat there. *What just happened? Have I turned a monster loose?* Suddenly he jumped up and ran after Judas, catching up with him before he reached the street.

"Wait," he said as he grabbed Judas' cloak. "I'll help you, but you must not cause any harm to come to Jesus."

Judas turned toward him, a smile on his face.

"I knew I could count on you," he said. "I'll tell you the full plan tomorrow."

The sun rose the next morning, to a beautiful day. A gentle breeze caressed Simon's face as he and Judas walked out of the city to the top of a small nearby hill. Bird calls from the mustard tree drew their attention. A flock of birds flew above them greeting the warmth of the sun with graceful maneuvers in the air. Simon took a deep breath as he sat on a rock and took in the whole scene. Judas turned to him and a sudden darkness fell on Simon's soul as he heard what he said.

"We are in Jerusalem. It is Passover. There are many people here and it will not be hard for you to slip away unnoticed. You will go to the Chief Priest and tell him that you are a Zealot who has been gathering information on Jesus. You would like to make a bargain with him – you will provide him access to Jesus at a time when He is away by Himself. Take whatever money he offers you, then tell him that you will send word when the time is right and personally lead him to Jesus. When he takes Him into custody, your mission ends.

"But," Simon pled, "what if he wants to kill him?"

"Do you not know that it is illegal for the Jews to put anyone to death for the kind of charges they could bring against Him?" Judas retorted, adding, "And, besides, Jesus won't let them take Him, for He could not give us our freedom if He loses His. If He is the Messiah, He cannot let that happen, don't you see?"

"I see that I cannot do this thing you ask," Simon replied.

"You are a coward," Judas growled. "I will show you how a hero acts. This plan will work and will bring about the end we both desire – freedom and the new kingdom of Israel. Watch and see." He strode sharply away.

Simon's heart ached as he watched Judas descend the hill. Slowly, he stood up and looked around. There were no birds singing now. No clouds were in the sky. The sun was bright around him, but there was a chill in his heart. As he returned to the city, he decided that he would tell Jesus what Judas was plotting. *I waited for the right time, but I waited too long.*

That evening, Jesus and the disciples celebrated the Passover Feast in an upper room in the city. As they ate, Jesus told them many things and prayed for them. Then He startled them saying,

"Truly, truly, I say to you, one of you will betray me." They all looked at one another. The others were uncertain of whom he spoke, but Simon was afraid that *he* knew. John, who was reclining beside Jesus, leaned back and said to Him,

"Lord, who is it?" Jesus answered, "It is he to whom I

will give this morsel of bread when I have dipped it." So when he had dipped the morsel, he gave it to Judas, the son of Simon Iscariot. When Judas took the morsel, Simon saw Judas' face change and his heart sank. Jesus said to Judas,

"What you are going to do, do quickly." *I didn't ever tell Jesus of Judas' plan, but He knew! He must have known all along, but how? Jesus had to be the Messiah! But if He was, why did he die? Why didn't God show His mighty power? Why didn't He save Jesus so He could lead us to victory and restore our nation? Was I supposed to do something to keep this from happening? Am I responsible for upsetting God's plan?*

Now, standing alone on a starlit hillside at Bethany, Simon despised himself for not doing anything at all. *Perhaps I could have stopped it.* He recalled the events that followed. *Judas had carried out his plan. Later that evening, Jesus left the rest of us in a camp near the entrance to the Garden of Gethsemane where many visitors to Jerusalem camped at night. Taking Peter, James and John, Jesus went deeper into the garden to pray, as He often did. After some time, a troop of Temple Guards, led by Judas, passed by near us.*

Seeing the procession, I knew what Judas was doing — leading them to the Master, so I tried to get ahead of them through the trees to warn Jesus and the others, but I was too late. I got there just as Judas kissed Jesus on the cheek. I saw Peter attempt to defend the Master with his fisherman's knife. I saw Jesus reach down, retrieve and heal the ear Peter had cut off the head of one of the chief priest's servants. I saw the guards tie His hands and escort Jesus out of the garden and back to Jerusalem. But there was nothing I could do to stop it. The troop of guards was accompanied by a rowdy crowd who had followed them. I felt sick. I fell on the ground and prayed that God would intervene with legions of angels to defend the Messiah, as Judas expected, but He didn't.

Suddenly James was lifting me to my feet. He had seen me approach while the arrest was taking place. James had darted into the underbrush to avoid being arrested.

"We must leave right now, before they arrest us, too," he whispered. "Are the others still in camp?" I nodded and James continued, "Let's get them and go someplace where we can decide what to do next."

I was on my feet now. We ran back to the camp, rousing the others and silently directing them to follow as we led them up the mountain toward Bethany. When we had covered a fair distance, I looked back and saw the retreating torches. Knowing then that we were not the objects of a further search, I bade the others to sit and rest while we decided what to do next. The decision was made to go to Bethany and wait until the next day. Surely nothing of any consequence would be done until morning and we would have a plan by then. But the next day, we were still so afraid that we were unable to agree on any action, so we stayed through the Sabbath where we had often stayed before – at the home of Mary, Martha and Lazarus.

Later, we heard that Judas, feeling guilty for the betrayal, confronted the chief priest the next morning after Pilate sentenced Jesus to death. He tried to give the money back to them, but they laughed at him and refused to take it. He was trying to redeem Jesus' life, but it was too late. While Jesus hung on the cross and we hid in fear for our lives, Judas bought a rope, went out into a field and hanged himself.

Simon tasted the bitter tears of remorse running down his cheeks. *I, too, betrayed the Messiah by my inaction. Judas called me a coward and, indeed, I am. What can I ever do to pay for my misdeeds? Jesus had offered me forgiveness – the only way to have peace – and now He is gone. Now he is lost forever. What did I do? Nothing! What could I have done?* This was a question that would haunt him forever. Simon hung his head in shame.

Mary of Magdala

Psalm 107:1-2
Oh give thanks to the Lord, for he is good,
for his steadfast love endures forever!
Let the redeemed of the Lord say so,
whom he has redeemed from trouble.

Mary sat in the corner of the dismal rented room she shared with several of the women who followed Jesus. Although the sun was still in the Sabbath sky, this place was gloomy. The sparse furnishings had been used for many years and bore the marks of little upkeep. But maybe it was the brightness outside that made the darkness of her mood more pronounced.

As Mary Magdalene contemplated the events of the past few days, her emptiness overwhelmed her – the loss of the One who had done so much for her and on Whom she had placed all her hopes. She knew the taste of this morose feeling. She had tasted it before. It was the flavor of total emptiness and she drank its full cup the day before she met the Man who had changed her life.

She felt the tears running down her cheeks as she remembered how skeptical she had been when she first met Jesus. *He asked me if I really wanted to be freed from those evil spirits which inhabited my body. How could I not want to be rid of them? All of my life they had caused me to do things I didn't want to do.*

Her mother died in the childbirth of her fourth son when Mary was six years old. Soon after that her father married another woman, who detested the lone girl in the family. She treated Mary as a servant rather than a daughter and, because her father was so stern and his punishments so harsh, she had become rebellious.

"You are never going to amount to anything, you worthless child! You won't ever find a husband to put up with you. You aren't even comely enough to be a harlot." She still flinched as she remembered those words. Her father shouted them after her as she ran out the door, her bare feet flying across the stone-filled hillside into the unknown world. *The sting of those words made me do a lot of wrong things,* she thought.

Her rebellious nature had sent her out into a hostile world far too early. It still hurt that her father had not even looked for her. *If that was all he cared about me, I'm well rid of him. I'll never return. I'll make my own life and show him that I'm not worthless!*

So she had found her way to Magdala, a village on the Sea of Galilee. She begged for her food and lived in a small cave just outside of the village. On a few rare occasions, one of the village women gave her some cast off clothing. Her life was difficult and cruel for the next five years, but she survived and became hardened to it. One afternoon as Mary was drawing water to take to her cave, one of the village harlots came to the well.

"Did you run out of water this morning?" the woman asked her. Mary concentrated on the jar she was lowering.

"Perhaps your mother needed extra water to wash some

clothes," the woman continued. Mary began pulling up the heavy water-filled jar. She wasn't used to having people talk to her and yet, she longed for someone to care about her. This woman at least spoke in a kind voice that did not seem to judge her.

"No," Mary replied, looking down at her dirty, coarsely spun tunic and her bare feet. "My mother is dead."

"Do you live with your father?" the woman asked.

"No," Mary answered, emphatically stamping a bare foot on the dusty ground. "I will never live with him again. He hates me."

"Surely you don't mean that," she sympathized.

"But I do!" shouted Mary, "He called me 'worthless'."

"I can see that you are not worthless," the woman replied. "I'll bet you know how to work, even as small as you are. Are you living with anyone?"

"No," Mary answered tentatively, wondering where this was leading.

"Would you like to live with me?" the woman asked. "I have a nice home and you could live with me and help me with housework and learn to cook."

Mary looked at her for the first time. *She is dressed in a tunic of fine linen and she has a multi-colored cloak draped around her. On her feet are leather sandals and her hair is covered by a silken veil. She wore these fine clothes to fetch water,* Mary thought. *Maybe working for her would not be so bad.*

"What would your husband think about me coming into your household?" Mary asked.

"I have no husband. I live alone," the woman answered. Mary was surprised. *She wants me to come into her home.*

"Yes," Mary finally said, "I will work for you – at least for a while."

"I'm glad," responded the now smiling woman. "My name is Ada. Come, let us go home."

Mary did the cleaning up each morning. She felt that now she was special for Ada had chosen her to live with her in her home. It was a large three room house and filled with lovely things. One room was set aside for Ada's "business" – it was the most finely appointed room in the house – draped with silken scarves and a fine bed covered with numerous pillows. Mary carefully arranged items on the shelves in the central room as Ada had shown her. She quickly learned how to prepare a tasty repast for the woman's guests. When Ada entertained her guests, Mary peeked through a slit in the curtain and listened as the woman plied her trade. She saw how generously she was rewarded. Mary stored in her mind all she heard and all the rest of the details.

As she grew into womanhood, Mary realized that her father had been very wrong. She *did* attract men's attention. If she looked flirtatiously at a man, he would come to her. She had learned well from observing her mentor what to do to please men, so one day she approached Ada.

"I have been here long enough," Mary began.

"And now you want to try your own wings," Ada picked up her thought. "I understand. I, too, came to this point when I was your age."

"I have learned many things in this house," Mary stated, "but now I want to make my own way. I am so grateful that you rescued me from living in the cave, but now you have shown me a better life and I want it for myself."

"You could stay here and make your life as an equal with me," Ada offered.

"No, it wouldn't work," Mary responded. "I have about

thought about it and I fear that if we were to be in competition in the same house, our wonderful friendship would turn ugly. I wouldn't want that. I must go."

"Perhaps you are right! So much wisdom from such a small one! Are you sure you can make it on your own?"

"Yes," Mary answered, "for a long time I have been saving the coins you have given me and now I have enough to start with. I'll be fine," she assured Ada.

The older woman held both of Mary's shoulders and looked her over from head to toe. She had grown to love this girl and she felt a certain pride in her. She was plucky and would make her way. Although Ada was sad to see her leave her company, she admired Mary's decision.

"Well, let's see if you have enough clothing to begin a new life," she said as she took Mary's hand and went to the chest of clothing. She took out a tunic and held it up to Mary's shoulders. Satisfied, she handed it to the girl. She reached in again, pulled out a sash and a multi-colored cloak and gave them to her. Ada walked to the wall and took a bright-colored veil from it, placing it also in Mary's hand. Reaching down, she picked up a pair of sandals and handed them to her. When she was satisfied with the wardrobe she had placed in Mary's arms, she embraced her, kissed her cheek and bade her goodbye.

Going to the other side of town, Mary found a small house by the heavily-travelled road from Capernaum where she could start her own business. It wasn't hard to entice men to come in to her, and when the man had satisfied himself, he would usually give her nice things – food, money, clothing or trinkets.

A few times, she was unable to please the man. Those men didn't give her anything but bruises. She supposed that was a part of the business she would have to put up with. She noticed that a few of the men she had seen with Ada were now coming to her, but she didn't think much of it. She had done nothing to draw them away from Ada. They had made their own choice.

Soon she had enough money to rent a fine two room house in the village, which made it easier for the men to come. She now dressed in enticing clothes she had bought. Her shelves held many of the trinkets she had received and she always had a fine table set for her guests to enjoy if they wanted something to eat. She felt successful, but there was a longing inside her for something more – true caring – something she had never known.

The women of the village avoided her completely, so she went to the well in the afternoon, when the village women were busy doing other chores. If they saw her, they spat at her and turned their backs. They knew that many of their husbands called upon her at one time or another. That didn't bother Mary. It was all worth it. She had proved her father wrong. She was now told by many men that she was beautiful and she believed it.

She thought she had a friend in Ada, but recently she had met her at the well. Ada's accusation that Mary was purposely stealing her men had cut her to the bone. *I don't want to harm in any way the woman who helped me when I really needed it, but the fact is that that is the way it is. The men are making their own choice. Who needs friends anyway,* she thought. *I have company every night – at least for part of every night.*

Then one day, a young rabbi traveled through Magdala. Mary was standing at her door as He passed. She didn't say anything, only smiled flirtatiously as she had done to other rabbis and priests. Many of them had come to her at night after such an invitation, but this Man seemed to be different. He looked at her and smiled, but His smile was not like other men's. There was no lust in it. Instead, she felt overpowering warmth fill her and an intense desire to see what he was teaching. She pondered this strange feeling all through that day and night. *The men last night didn't give me the same comfort as before. I no longer want to flirt with men and this business suddenly seems unimportant to me. I feel so alone and desolate – so unloved – only used.*

This home with all its fine trappings, the fine pieces of pottery I have acquired, the lovely cloaks and veils hanging from pegs on the wall was how I always thought I wanted to live. I have proved that I am what my father said I could not be. But now I see that is really nothing – nothing that truly matters. If I would die tonight, who would care? Maybe all I ever had were dreams. But maybe what I really want is love – unconditional love. Without that, what is life?

Suddenly seeing her life for what it was, she was aware of the bitter taste in her mouth. It was the flavor of complete solitude in the world – the taste of total loss. Mary sat down on the bed and cried. The smile the rabbi had cast her way made her feel valuable and loved while she was in it and she now realized that she wanted to feel that way again. *There must be more to life than what I have.* When He didn't come to her that night, she knew that He was different and decided what she must do.

Mary packed the money she had and a few belongings in a pouch, gathered a cloak about her and started off early the next morning in search of the rabbi, leaving everything else behind. Somehow, she just knew that if she could find him, her life would change. She gave no thought about making a living – only about finding a life.

The sun was high above when Mary reached Tagbha, a small fishing village. She was looking around for a place she could sit down and eat some of the dates and nuts she had thought to put in her pouch. There he was! Standing before a large crowd by the lake, teaching them. Suddenly, her hunger was not for dates and nuts. Not wanting to call attention to herself, she made her way through a small grove of trees, stopped a short way behind the last row, and listened. He was saying remarkable things to the people.

"Love your enemies," He said, "do good and lend, expecting nothing in return, and your reward will be great."

Never had Mary heard such words. *How can He say such things?* Then she heard words she was sure were spoken just for her.

"Judge not, and you will not be judged. Condemn not and you shall not be condemned. Forgive and you will be forgiven." *My heart is bursting with a desire for forgiveness for all the things I have been doing. Things that I now realize are sinful. 'Evil spirits cause sins', my father yelled at me when he accused me of wrongdoing. I must be possessed by an evil spirit.* At that moment, she knew she must meet this rabbi face to face.

From the edge of the crowd, she watched the faces of the listeners. They were carefully absorbing every word, all except the Pharisees standing near her who were observing Jesus critically. On their faces were looks of contempt – the same contempt she saw when they looked at her. She knew their vile thoughts, for the same kind of men had come to her house by the light of the moon. *They put on such proper airs, but they are rotten inside. They are no better than anyone else – in fact, they are much worse than most men. They pass judgment on others in public for the very things of which they are most guilty in secret.*

When Jesus finished speaking, He and His followers started walking toward Capernaum. Mary pushed through the crowd which was following Him as if they could not get enough of His teaching. The procession was almost to their destination when she finally caught up with Jesus through the crowd.

"Teacher," she implored when she got close enough, "can you help me?" Jesus stopped and Mary bowed at His feet and wept. "I am troubled by an evil spirit from my birth and it has caused me to do many sinful things. Can You drive the spirit from me? Will You free me from it?"

"I can and I will," Jesus answered with a compassionate smile. He placed His hands on her head and, calling it by name, commanded the spirit to leave. Although it left her, Jesus' hands remained on her head. Six more times, He called other spirits by name and each left her body at His command. She was totally exhausted and slumped to the ground, sobbing.

Jesus knelt beside her, placing His hand on her heaving shoulder. Mary tried to look up at Him, blinking back the tears. She attempted to speak, but couldn't find her voice. It took a while for her to rise to a sitting position. Jesus smiled at her and in a few more minutes His hands took hers and He gently raised her to her feet.

"There, my daughter," He said, "your faith has freed you from the spirits which have plagued you. Go your way and do not sin. Remember what the psalmist told us, 'When my father and mother forsake me, then the Lord will take care of me.' You will never be alone."

"Master," she pled, "I cannot leave you. I must know more of your wisdom. I will serve you in whatever manner I am able. May I continue to follow you?"

"Your service to My Father will be welcome," He told her. Mary's heart nearly burst with joy as she heard these life-giving words.

"From this moment on," she vowed, "I will serve You with all that I am." She wasn't sure whether the warmth she felt was from the sun, or from her glowing heart, but it was a feeling she wanted to have for the rest of her life.

And she followed Him for two and a half years, doing whatever she could to serve His ministry to others. She had used her money for provisions and yet, there always seemed to be as much after she spent some as there was before. She had prepared food for the disciples daily. Her garb changed from gaudy raiment to the plain clothes of ordinary women and her language lost all of its colorful vulgarity. The other women who followed Jesus treated her with love, not judgment. She felt the acceptance she had been longing for all of her life. Jesus had not only freed her from the evil spirits, but following and serving Him opened up a whole new world to her. She was no longer simply existing, but truly living. Her life, at last, had real value.

Her heart warmed at the thoughts of those times, but now she found herself in this gloomy room, knowing that she would no longer be able to serve the Master. He had been crucified and, now, buried in a borrowed tomb behind a huge stone. Her loneliness and desolation at this realization immobilized her. *What had happened in the course of just a couple of days?*

Only two days ago she helped prepare the Passover meal for Jesus and His disciples and they ate it as on previous Passovers. Afterward, as He often did, Jesus took the men with Him to the Garden of Gethsemane where they could pray in private. Mary and the other women cleared the table and cleaned up the room, then went to the smaller room next to the larger room in which several of the disciples were staying. The other women left to stay with relatives for the Sabbath. About the time Mary was lying down to sleep, she faintly heard angry voices and marching feet in the distance. There are so many people in the city at this festival time. Something is always going on, she thought as her eyes closed in sleep.

When dawn came, Mary arose to begin preparations for the day's activities. A knock on the door surprised her and when she opened it, she was even more surprised to see Joanna, wife of King Herod's steward, standing there.

"You haven't heard?" Joanna asked, seeing Mary's face.

"No, what?" she asked.

"They arrested Jesus," Joanna answered.

"Arrested Him?" Mary gasped. "Why? Where? Who?"

"The Temple Guard and a bunch of the town thugs were led to Him by Judas Iscariot – the traitor!" Joanna responded.

"Where did they take Him?" Mary pressed. *I'll go to Him.*

"I don't know."

Mary left her work and went with Joanna to seek Jesus.

They first went to the Temple, but He wasn't there. Joanna stopped Mary.

"It is dangerous to go on," she said, "I must return home before my husband discovers my absence. You had better abandon the search, too."

Mary nodded in agreement and Joanna disappeared around a corner. Suddenly aware of shouting coming from the area of the Praetorium, where the Roman governor lived in Jerusalem and the Roman garrison was headquartered, Mary went in that direction. She did not fear for her life, for all of her life was in Jesus. *I must find Him!* The tower of the Praetorium rose above Temple Mount so that the Romans could look down into the courtyards of the Temple to watch the Jews in case something was brewing that might lead to rebellion.

Mary walked toward the wall surrounding Temple Mount so she could hear what they were saying. She was horrified to hear the crowd shouting "Crucify Him! Crucify Him!" *Who is standing before them? Can it be Jesus? Are they calling for Jesus' crucifixion? Surely not! What crime has He ever committed? He is a man of peace. He says, "Love your enemies. Do good to those who spitefully use you."*

She turned to leave the Temple courtyard. The nearest available gate was on the opposite side of the Temple and by the time she went around the inner courtyards to that gate, she could hear that the tone of the mob had changed to one of increasing violence. Mary reached the street and asked a woman who was passing by what was happening.

"Pontius Pilate just freed Barrabas," she told her, adding, "we need another murderer on the streets. We'd better go home."

"The Romans free a prisoner every Passover," Mary replied.

"Yes, and this year," the woman interrupted, "Pilate gave the crowd a choice – Barrabas or the Man they call Jesus."

"And they freed Barrabas?" Mary could hardly say the words. *How could there have been such a choice – a murderer or a Man of peace and love?* Her mind raced as she asked the woman,

"And what is to become of Jesus?"

"He is to be crucified. He will be coming this way after He is scourged," she answered. Mary sunk to her knees against the wall of the house and raised her eyes to heaven. Her voice could not be heard by those passing, but tears streamed down her face as she quietly prayed.

"Heavenly Father," she pleaded, "is this your plan? That your Son would die? So soon? This terrible way? Doesn't He have much more to do on this earth? What will we who followed Him these years do? What will happen to us? Are we to die, too? Or will we have to return to our former lives? Many of us gave up everything – possessions, family, home – to follow Him. We are so sure that Jesus is the promised Messiah. Is this Your plan for the Messiah? "Did He come for just a short time? For many generations, we have lived on the promise of His coming. Surely this can't be the end of it! Father, aren't You going to do something? Won't You stop it from happening? Please, Lord, don't let it come to pass! Send Your angels to stop this terrible thing. I don't want to ever return to what I was. I can't! Oh, Lord, have mercy – on Him – on us all!"

She could hear the mob again raising their voices as they came nearer, taunting prisoners being taken to the Damascus Gate and the place of their deaths. Arising to follow the throng, she moved as quickly as she could. Many people had come out of their houses to see what all the noise was about and the streets were full of them.

Roman soldiers appeared and began shoving spectators back into doorways and side streets. Then came the prisoners.

Mary was heartened when she saw first one man and then another and neither of them was the Rabbi. But, then she saw Him – the third man – so badly beaten and bloody that she barely recognized Him!

What have they done to Him? Why are they so cruelly mistreating this man who only showed love for all mankind? Don't they know who

He is? What can I do for Him? There must be something! The crowd followed behind the procession, jostling and shoving one another. The whole thing sickened Mary. She slumped down in the doorway next to where she had been standing and wept until most of the crowd shoved past before she followed them.

By the time Mary got to Golgotha, the Place of the Skull, the most prominent location in miles of crucifixion sites near Jerusalem, all three men had been raised on crosses. The two other men had been tied to their crosses so that their deaths would be more prolonged. They would experience extreme mental anguish as they slowly suffocated when constantly raising and lowering their body in order to breathe brought them to exhaustion.

Jesus had been treated differently. His hands were extended on the cross beam and large nails through the base of His hands secured them. His feet were overlapped and held with another nail. He was so bloody! It dripped from the wounds where a crown made of thorns had been jammed down on the head already badly bruised from the beating He had endured. Streams of blood flowed from His back, from the thirty-nine lashes he had received from a cruel Roman whip. Droplets fell from the nails piercing His hands and feet.

She couldn't watch as He pushed His body up to get a breath. Tears flooded her eyes and clouds of darkness covered her heart, yet she couldn't move from the place. She looked around her and saw John standing with Jesus' mother, Mary, at the foot of the cross where He hung. Several other women who had known and followed Him were standing on a small rise by the road. Going to them, she didn't feel so alone. No one spoke a word. She knelt and, with her head bowed, prayed.

"Heavenly Father, how You must be grieving, seeing

Your Son upon this cruel cross. I don't understand how You could let Him undergo such suffering. He was with us for so short a time and He could have done so much more for us. What can He do in death? Oh, Lord, hear my prayer. Is this the end? What's to become of us now? I don't know how to go on living without Him. Help me, Lord, help us all!"

In midafternoon, the next day being the Sabbath, the soldiers received orders to hurry the three deaths, so two of them, carrying large mallets, came to the two criminals. Raising the mallets, they swung them at the two men, breaking their legs with the impact. When they could no longer lift their bodies to breathe, they would die sooner. Having completed the task on the first two, the soldiers both went to Jesus, but discovered that He was already dead, so they lowered the mallets and turned away. Hearing the soldiers' pronouncement of death, Mary saw an older man who had been observing, quickly confer with a companion, then both of them turned from the scene and purposefully set out in the direction of the Praetorium.

When the women saw John help Jesus' mother to her feet, they knew that He had died. Mary was filled with the desire to go to them and help her. As she took the first step, she felt a hand on her arm.

"No, Mary, I will go to her. She is my sister," Salome firmly stated and Mary nodded her head in assent. Salome was also John's mother and both of them would need her steady strength now. When the trio was out of sight, Mary's gaze returned to the cross. A Roman soldier approached Jesus and thrust a spear into His side. Out came a gush of water and blood. Mary turned her head and wept. When she looked back again, the soldier was gone. Still she couldn't leave the place. Her Master was there and she couldn't leave Him.

The crowd was dispersing when one of the two older men returned and approached the center cross with something in his arms. He was followed by two men carrying ladders, which they placed against each side of the cross. The two men climbed the ladders and removed the crossbeam. Quickly, they retreated down the ladders and laid the beam down.

While they were climbing up, the older man had removed the nail which secured Jesus' feet and they dangled limply. As the men lowered the crossbeam, the man on the ground gently gathered the bruised and bleeding legs and the body was laid out on the ground. The nails securing Jesus' hands were removed.

The two who had been on the ladder gently lifted the Lord's body and placed it on one of the ladders. As they carried it off, the older man, carrying a bundle of cloth and the second ladder, followed. Just then, the other man returned, carrying a large, heavy sack on his back, and followed them. Mary followed at a distance. This was unusual and she wanted to know what these men were doing. *Are they stealing Jesus' body? Why?*

Mary followed them to an unfinished tomb in a nearby garden. The men carried Jesus' body inside. Then the two younger men came outside to wait near the opening. The older men were still inside when four Roman soldiers and their captain arrived to take up watch. When the men came out some time later, all nine of them moved the stone across the doorway to the tomb. Producing a seal, the captain applied it to the stone, securing the body inside. The soldiers took up their positions. Mary left ahead of the men, because the sun was now sinking behind the hills, signaling that the Sabbath was nigh. All the way back to her lodging, Mary wept. She felt so lost now. She feared that the spirits Jesus had cast out of her would return. *What would I do then? I don't want lose the close associations I have with the other women. Neither do I want to return to the hollow life I led before I met Him.* She cried until no more tears were left. Exhausted and spent, she laid down on her mat in the gloomy room and let the darkness of her mood overtake her, mourning in solitude.

The Sabbath had been a God-ordained day of worship and rest for Mary since she first began to follow Jesus, but she hadn't rested this day. Her grief hadn't let her. Peter had returned to the larger room while she was gone but he remained alone there through the Sabbath, neither eating nor drinking, — completely engulfed with his grief. It had been good for them both to have this God-appointed day of rest in which to mourn.

Now it was dark outside. She roused herself. The long, lonely Sabbath had finally come to an end. None of the other women had returned to the room yet. Mary didn't know if they ever would. Perhaps they had fled for their lives. Even Peter has gone somewhere, she thought as she heard the outer door close.

During her prayers at sunset, Mary received an inspiration and now she would act upon it. There was still one more thing she could do for her Lord – dress His body with spices and oils – a last labor of love. When darkness fell and Sabbath was over, she gathered Joanna, Salome, the wife of Zebedee, and another Mary and they all went to the home which was the followers' meeting place. That evening the five women, including the owner of the house, collected and prepared spices and oil to take to the tomb when morning broke.

"What will we do about moving the stone?" Salome asked.

"The Lord will be with us," Mary confidently stated.

89

Nicodemus, Pharisee

1 John 2:11
But whoever hates his brother is in the darkness and walks in the darkness, and does not know where he is going, because the darkness has blinded his eyes.

He had been alone in his room since he returned from the tomb. Life was continuing outside his door. No one seemed to realize the terrible miscarriage of justice that had been perpetrated and carried out yesterday! *Why were they so blind? Could they not see that this action had been entirely wrong? Why did it take me so long to really see Jesus for who He truly was?*

Nicodemus was still reeling from the turn of events that had brought about the death of the man he now knew beyond doubt was truly a prophet of God – perhaps even the Son of God as He had claimed. *Why didn't I see the truth that night nearly three years ago when I went to see Him under the cover of darkness? Why did I allow myself to give more credence to the things I had learned all my life, than to the amazing person I now, at last, recognize could be God's only Son?* He wanted more than anything to speak with Jesus. But now it was too late! He was gone – crucified by the Romans at the insistence of the Sanhedrin, of which he was a revered member.

Sadly, Nicodemus remembered his first conversation with Jesus. His cowardice had governed him even then for he sought Him out under the cover of darkness so that no one would see him. His position on the Sanhedrin, the governing body consisting of priests and the two powerful political parties, Pharisees and Sadducees, was all-important to him. Still, something had led him to speak personally with this popular rabbi. *I want the things Jesus said to be true. If they are true, why did He meet with opposition?*

He remembered the wind tearing at his garments as he stole through the dark streets that gusty spring night. Clouds scudded across the sky partially obscuring the quarter moon for a few moments at a time.

He had learned that Jesus was staying in a rooftop room at the house of Jacob, the carpenter. Grateful for the privacy afforded by the outside stairs leading to the rooftop, Nicodemus quietly climbed up. As he reached the top, he saw Jesus kneeling near the wall. His arms were spread wide and He looked heavenward as He prayed. Nicodemus stepped onto the roof. A loose tile signaled his presence and after a few minutes more in prayer, Jesus lowered His arms and turned, looking at him and smiling.

"Rabbi," Nicodemus addressed Him, "we know that You are a teacher come from God; for no one can do these signs that You do unless God is with him."

"Truly, truly, I say to you," Jesus responded, "unless one is born again he cannot see the kingdom of God."

"How can a man be born when he is old?" Nicodemus asked. *I know that when a gentile converts to Judaism and is baptized, he is considered a "new creature," but I also know that this is not what Jesus is saying, so I will continue challenging Jesus with my unbelief,* "Can he enter a second time into his mother's womb and be born?"

"Truly, truly, I say to you, unless one is born of water and the Spirit, he cannot enter the kingdom of God," Jesus explained. "That which is born of the flesh is flesh and that which is born of the Spirit is spirit." Jesus saw the look of puzzlement on his learned questioner's face.

"Do not marvel that I said to you, 'You must be born again.' The wind blows where it wishes," Jesus said, gesturing as a hearty gust rushed past, "and you hear its sound, but you do not know where it comes from and where it goes. So it is with everyone who is born of the Spirit."

"How can these things be?" Nicodemus puzzled aloud. *I know the teaching of the prophets, but I can't accept the thought that I, a Pharisee, need to change. I lead a righteous life, following the law exactly.*

"Are you a teacher of Israel and yet you do not understand these things?" Jesus asked and then continued. "Most assuredly, I say to you, We speak what We know and testify what We have seen, and you do not receive Our witness. If I told you earthly things and you do not believe, how will you believe if I tell you heavenly things? No one has ascended to heaven but He who came down from heaven." Nicodemus was taken aback! *It sounds like this rabbi is claiming to be the Son of God! How could that be? He is only a simple rabbi from Galilee.*

Jesus paused to let the things He had said sink into the man's mind and heart before continuing, speaking slowly, and pausing frequently, "And as Moses lifted up the serpent in the wilderness, so must the Son of Man be lifted up, that whoever believes in him may have eternal life.

"For God so loved the world, that he gave his only Son, that whoever believes in him should not perish but have eternal life, for God did not send his Son into the world to condemn the world, but in order that the world might be saved through Him. Whoever believes in Him is not condemned, but whoever does not believe is condemned already, because he has not believed in the name of the only Son of God. And this is the judgment: the light has come into the world, and people loved the darkness rather than the light because their works were evil. For everyone who does wicked things hates the light and does not come to the light, lest his works should be exposed. But whoever does what is true comes to the light, so that it may be clearly seen that his works have been carried out in God."

Nicodemus stood there, staring at Jesus, his mind struggling to absorb all that Jesus had said. Finally, he took a step toward the stairway. Putting his arm around the older man's shoulders, Jesus walked with him to the steps. Silently, they parted company.

Nicodemus returned to his home and spent most of the night and the next day pondering this conversation. *I still did not fully understand all of it, but I did begin to see some of the meaning of the teaching I received that night. Now and again, pieces have come to mind since then and little by little, as I became aware of how much my life does fall short of the perfection I seek, I began to make changes.*

Looking back, I can see that I should have stood more firmly in Jesus' defense before the Sanhedrin – made them understand the consequences of what they were bent on doing – kept them from the terrible deed that will surely condemn their souls forever to the fires of hell. I knew then that I did not fully understood all that Jesus said to me, but now I know that I did not even begin to understand it until I stood at the foot of the cross.

Still, he had been sure enough of the goodness of Jesus and his ministry to stand up once in the Sanhedrin when officers, sent out to bring Jesus to the council, came back empty-handed.

"Why have you not brought Him?" the Pharisees demanded.

"No man ever spoke like this Man," one officer responded.

"Are you also deceived?" one of the Pharisees scoffed. "Have any of the rulers or the Pharisees believed in Him?"

"But this crowd that does not know the law is accursed," said another Pharisee.

"Does our law judge a man before it hears him and knows what he is doing?" ventured Nicodemus as he stood up. He saw the tenor of the assembly change. One of the Pharisees, glared at him as he spat out his venomous retort.

"Are you also from Galilee? Search and look, for no prophet has arisen out of Galilee."

Nicodemus had no answer to that assertion, so he sat down. *I know the Scripture, and surely, there is an answer to that comment in it, but I do not know it at this crucial time.*

His reluctance to go against the priests, Pharisees and Sadducees on several occasions had most likely sealed Jesus' fate, too. *It was not until I saw Jesus hanging from that hateful cross that the full realization of the terrible result of my reluctance to declare for Him burst on my mind. I allowed these men to kill the Man who I now believe was God's Son! Why was I so weak and fearful of men? Shouldn't my fear have been of God? I was in a position to present the defense for Jesus – but I didn't. I had the standing and the wealth to influence those in power – but I didn't. Instead, in my reluctance, I allowed their jealousy and hatred of the Man who could change the world to be fanned into a fire that devoured Him in death. I can never forgive myself!*

Although he had searched for verification of Jesus' birthplace, he still did not know the answer to the question, but yet, as he gazed at the cross, he had come to truly believe that

Jesus was the Son of God. That was why, as he witnessed the crucifixion drawing to an end in the late afternoon, he sought out another member of the Sanhedrin who was also witnessing this travesty and who also believed on Jesus. Joseph of Arimathea was his name and he had even greater wealth and influence. When he saw that Jesus was dead, Nicodemus approached him.

"Joseph," Nicodemus began, "they have succeeded – they have killed Him."

"Indeed they have. Although I did not join in that action, I am so ashamed to have been a part of the body that convicted Him," Joseph stated.

"I am, too," Nicodemus agreed, "but perhaps there is something we can still do. I will locate a burial site and we can claim His body."

"You need not search," said Joseph in a moment of inspiration. "I know of a tomb that is ready and nearby."

"Will the owner agree to our use of it to hold Jesus' body?" Nicodemus asked.

"Most assuredly! It is mine," Joseph answered. "I commissioned it made in the garden right over there for my family. It is near enough finished that it would be suitable."

"That would be wonderful, but are you certain?" Nicodemus pressed.

"Yes, it was probably God's will that I had it built," Joseph assured him. "I will have another made later. Come, we must hurry to claim the body so that we can finish the burial before the beginning of Sabbath."

Together they went to Pilate to request permission to receive Jesus' body for burial.

Pontius Pilate was the harsh administrator of Roman

interests in Palestine. He had risen to his post through a strategic marriage and merciless actions. He was certainly no lover of the Jews, considering them to be crude peasants good only for the taxes they were required to pay. He worked with the Chief Priest, who was in essence the leader of the Jews.

Their "king" was appointed by the Romans to ease the problem of maintaining the peace in Jerusalem. That way Pilate could spend the majority of his time in the more pleasant port city of Caesarea. However, large festivals like the Passover required his presence in the capital city. The vast number of pilgrims who came at those times posed a threat of rebellion. And so Pilate was in residence at Antonia Fortress when the two men came with their plea for the release to them of the body of the Man, Jesus. The procurator was amazed that Jesus had died so quickly and sent a soldier to ascertain this truth. Joseph and Nicodemus were dismissed to an anteroom to await his return.

"Don't worry, Nicodemus," Joseph assured him, "Pilate will be glad to have the body taken off his hands. Be patient, my friend." *I knew that he was right, but I am always uneasy when I must deal with the Romans. One never knows what to expect.*

When the two men were again ushered into the main room, they saw the soldier who had been dispatched approaching Pilate. He bowed and stood at attention. Acknowledging the entrance of the two petitioning Jews, Pilate addressed the soldier.

"What was your finding?"

"The man is dead. His legs were not broken as the others' were, so I verified His death by piercing his side with my spear. Blood and water immediately gushed from the wound."

Nicodemus gasped as a prophecy from Scripture came

to his mind. *The Messianic Psalm 34 says "Not one of His bones shall be broken."*

"Well, then," said Pilate to the two Jews, "I see no reason your request cannot be granted. Make haste to rid us of one more problem."

"Thank you, my lord," Joseph replied and the two men bowed and left the fortress.

Quickly they set to work. Joseph went to buy a burial shroud and hire some workers to remove Jesus from the cross and carry his body to the tomb. Nicodemus went to the spice merchant and soon joined Joseph en route to the tomb with a large bag of spices on his back and a jug of oil in his hand. The oil would anoint the body. The spices were intended to disguise the stench of decaying flesh. These would fill the folds of the shroud according to custom.

Joseph carefully spread the shroud on the bed carved into the stone on the left side of the tomb. The workers laid the body on it. Joseph told them to wait outside the tomb. The two men hurried to complete their task as the sun was rapidly dropping behind the hills, signaling the beginning of the Sabbath.

After anointing Jesus' body with the oil, Nicodemus put scoops of spices alongside and atop the precious body. Joseph took a fine linen napkin from the voluminous sleeve of his robe and opened it. He kissed it and lovingly laid it across the face of the rabbi. Then the two men took the long loose end of the shroud and drew it over the body. More spices were added to the top of the covering and worked into the folds. Seeing that their work was complete, the two men stood side by side and prayed over the body of Jesus.

The sun was slipping past the horizon when they, the waiting workers and newly-arrived Roman guards rolled the heavy stone across the opening, then the tomb was sealed. At the insistence of the high priest, Pilate had assigned a watch of soldiers to stand guard in case Jesus' followers tried to steal the body and represent Him as being alive. The guard unit set up a makeshift camp at the site. Joseph paid the workers and they all left, leaving only the Roman soldiers.

There is no doubt in my mind that Jesus is truly dead. His body had grown cold and was stiffening as we dressed it in the tomb. The Pharisee had not attended his Sabbath duties at the Temple because he and Joseph were both unclean from tending to Jesus' dead body, so he had remained at home – in seclusion. He found himself wondering – *Did I misplace my belief that Jesus was the Son of God. Wouldn't the Son of God be immortal, eternal? Would God let Him die, especially the ignominious death to which Jesus had been subjected? Why would God allow such a thing to happen?*

Finally he fell on his face, praying for God's guidance.

"Show me Your truth, O Lord," he prayed, "I want to believe, but I am finding it so hard to accept that Jesus is the Messiah. The Messiah was to lead our people out of oppression, not to die the death of a criminal. Was this Your will, O Lord? Why did He die? O, Lord, I need to know, please show me Your truth…"

His prayer continued far into the night. Although he still didn't understand God's purpose, he had a strange peace about it all – as if God told him that it would all come together for good. He decided that he would wait for God's will to be revealed to him.

Mark, the Young Seeker

1 John 3:2
Beloved, we are God's children now, and what we will be has not yet appeared; but we know that when he appears we shall be like him, because we shall see him as he is.

Mark gazed out the window of his room at the heavens. As the stars popped out one by one in the darkening sky, his mind was filled with questions. He was so confused. So much had happened in the last few days and the questions kept coming. *I don't understand what it all means. My mother was so sure that the rabbi she heard at the Temple that day more than two years ago was the Messiah.*

She had been so happy when she came home that evening and told me about all that Jesus said when He was teaching. She was so certain, in fact, that the next day she met me at the synagogue school and had me accompany her back to the Temple so that I, too, could hear the wonderful teaching first hand.

The only times that I had been to the Temple before that were on the Sabbath, so I was amazed at the differences I saw on this mid-week visit. There were not as many money changers or sellers of animals and there seemed to be a lot more priests, but this might have been because there were not as many other people there this day. The priests were mostly standing in small groups at various places in the courtyard, discussing things with each other.

When Mother and I reached the area where Jesus sat teaching, there were a large number of people sitting around Him. Mother and I sat down at the back of the audience, listening as Jesus told one story after another and in between, He taught the truths of Scripture. I remember the story I thought was the best one that first day. I have carried it with me all the time since. Jesus was talking about how people said they believed Him, but didn't do the things He told them they should do. The story began with the part about the man who not only heard and believed, but acted upon his belief.

"I will show you what he is like," Jesus said. "He is like a man building a house, who dug deep and laid the foundation on the rock. And when a flood arose, the stream broke against that house and could not shake it, because it had been well built. But the one who hears and does not do what he hears is like a man who built a house on the ground without a foundation. When the stream broke against it, immediately it fell, and the ruin of that house was great."

When the teaching ended and the people were nearly gone, my mother approached Jesus. She looked down at the floor as she went and when she was near Him, Jesus reached out His hand and raised her head until she was looking directly into His eyes. I had never before seen my mother hesitant to speak, but she appeared to be so then.

"Is there something you want to ask Me?" the smiling Jesus said to her.

"Yes, Rabbi," she answered. "I want to invite you to stay at our house whenever you are in Jerusalem. It is a large house. We could host meetings there, if you want another place to teach. It would be our great honor if you would accept."

"I do accept your offer," Jesus replied.

"We will have the evening meal ready when You and your disciples arrive," Mary said.

"I'll look forward to sundown then," He told her and turned toward the disciples who were waiting a short distance away. *That was a pivotal point in my life for our home became a place where people came to meet even when Jesus wasn't in Jerusalem. And when He was there, it was always full!*

One night, Jesus was telling stories to the assembled crowd of followers gathered at our house. I was listening on the staircase to escape detection by my mother who had sent me to bed. I didn't want to miss anything Jesus said. Although it was late when the teaching ended, the disciples approached Jesus when they were alone and asked,

"Why do you speak to them in parables?" Jesus answered,

"To you it has been given to know the secrets of the kingdom of heaven, but to them it has not been given, for to the one who has, more will be given, and he will have an abundance, but from the one who has not, even what he has will be taken away. This is why I speak to them in parables, because seeing they do not see, and hearing they do not hear, nor do they understand.

"Indeed, in their case the prophecy of Isaiah is fulfilled that says: 'You will indeed hear but never understand, and you will indeed see but never perceive, for this people's heart has grown dull, and with their ears they can barely hear, and their eyes they have closed, lest they should see with their eyes and hear with their ears and understand with their heart and turn, and I would heal them.' But blessed are your eyes, for they see, and your ears, for they hear. For truly, I say to you, many prophets and righteous people longed to see what you see, and did not see it, and to hear what you hear, and did not hear it."

I listened to all Jesus said every time He came and when He left, I was always still hungry for more of His teaching, more of His truths, more of His presence.

The night of the Passover feast, many of the people celebrated the meal in Mark's home, but Jesus and His closest disciples had taken a secluded upper room in another home for a private time.

Mark, now considered to be a young man at fifteen years of age, enjoyed filling in as host in his father's absences while he conducted business. *I miss my father, who provides well for us by arranging for shipments of wood and copper from Cypress to Jerusalem. The wood is sold to wealthy families or to Herod for the interior of the Temple he is building and the copper becomes brass instruments or utensils also for the Temple. He is well-respected by his business connections and the whole community.* John Mark stepped into the role of protector for his mother when his father was on one of his frequent trips. But the part Mark liked best, was hosting a celebration.

After the lambs had been consumed and the rituals observed this Passover, the guests left for their lodgings and Mark and Mary retired for the night, leaving the servants to the work of cleaning up. The house was quiet and the hour was late when Mark was awakened by the sound of a crowd approaching the city gate. This was unusual for the gates were closed at sundown and not opened until sunup. Quickly he wrapped himself in the linen bed sheet and hurried to see what was happening.

It was a large group of rough-appearing people. *This strange crowd must be following someone on important business as the city gates are open allowing them to pass.* He slipped in among them, his curiosity driving him. Soon the gates closed behind them. Now the thought occurred to Mark -- *no one knows where I am and I might not be able to get back through the gates and to my bed before Mother comes to awaken me in the morning. She will be worried and rightly so.* Although he had celebrated his bar mitzvah a couple of years ago and was considered to be a man, his mother still thought of him as her boy and worried and fussed over him. But it was too late for him to have such thoughts now.

He worked his way to the edge of the crowd and looked as far ahead as he could. The torch-lit procession appeared to be headed by a company of soldiers – not Roman, but Temple guard. He could not imagine what they would be doing at this time of night. The lights from their torches turned into the Garden of Gethsemane. Then he could see only occasional flickers of light through the olive trees.

By the time the group collected where the soldiers had stopped and Mark found a place where he could observe without being noticed, he was astounded to see Jesus, the Master, bound and being pushed by the captain of the guard.

Where are the disciples, he wondered. The only one he saw was Judas Iscariot and he didn't seem to be under arrest. Mark let out a gasp and one of the ruffians heard him. He made a lunge at Mark and grabbed the sheet, but Mark let it go and ran from the place, naked. He stopped a short distance away when he saw that he wasn't being chased. After a few minutes, Mark saw the fellow throw the sheet aside as the crowd followed the Temple Guard taking Jesus out of the garden. When the crowd was gone, Mark retrieved the sheet, quickly wrapped it around himself and followed in the shadows.

Oh, Lord, please help me get home, he breathed. Several torches near the rear of the pack went out and the moonless night hid him as he worked his way into the edge of the men passing back through the city gates. With relief, he heard the muffled sound of the massive wooden gates as they closed again behind them. Now working his way to the edge of the crowd, he dropped into the deep darkness of a doorway. When the noise of the rabble was gone, Mark made his way back to his bed.

His mind was whirling with questions. *Why was Jesus arrested by the Temple Guard? Where are they taking Him? What will happen to Him? What could I have done to help Him? Should I awaken Mother and tell her about it?* He laid his head down on his pillow, but sleep evaded him the remainder of the night. As soon as he heard the servants stirring in the house, he put on a tunic and went to his mother's room.

"Mother," he said softly as he gently shook her shoulder. "Mother, I need to talk with you."

"At this hour?" Mary mumbled as her eyes opened, but she felt the trembling hand on her shoulder and knew immediately that something had frightened the boy.

"Yes, Mother," he began, "I disobeyed you this night and left my bed and this house. Please forgive my disobedience."

"Why did you do that?" she asked.

"I was awakened by the noise of a crowd in the street and went to see what it was about," he answered. Mary, now wide awake, listened as the lad told her about the frightening event of the night, ending with his most pressing question,

"Why did the Temple guard arrest the Messiah?"

"I don't know right now, but I will find out," she assured him, "Now, go back to bed and get some sleep. I'll tell the servants not to disturb you and when I know the answer, I'll awaken you." Mark obeyed his mother.

Mary was deeply worried. Quickly she dressed, put on her cloak, spoke with the housekeeper and left the house.

It was late afternoon when Mary returned. Mark had been awake for many hours. Her eyes were red and swollen. She had been weeping – an occasional sob still escaped. She slumped in a chair as Mark came to her side.

"What has happened, Mother?" queried a kneeling Mark.

"They have crucified Jesus," she sobbed.

"Crucified Him? Jesus? Why would they crucify Him? He never hurt anyone. He was gentle and kind. Who crucified Him?" Mark asked in anguish. His mother shook her head and buried it in her hands, sobbing. "The priests. It was the priests."

"Why would they do that? How could they? Isn't it illegal for them to put anyone to death?" Mark pleaded. Both of them cried for a time before Mary wiped her eyes and looked at her son. Her voice was strained, but steady as she explained.

"I was on the way to the Temple when I heard a crowd in front of the Praetorium. They were shouting "Crucify Him, Crucify Him."

"I saw the priests, even the High Priest, there urging the crowd to a frenzy. Pilate tried to release Jesus, even trying to free Him as the token prisoner he customarily frees at Passover. But when he saw that the crowd was so agitated and adamant, demanding that the murderer Barabbas be freed instead, he finally washed his hands in a bowl, signifying that he wanted nothing to do with this deed, and ordered Jesus' scourging and death.

"Then," she said, wringing her hands in helplessness, "I went to look for Nicodemus. I hoped that he would know what had happened and what we could do about it. I finally found him at his home. It took some persuasion to get him to talk with me. He was distraught, too. He had not been summoned to the house of Caiaphas in the wee hours of the morning with the rest of the Sanhedrin, probably because the others remembered that he had defended Jesus on previous occasions when they had discussed how to get rid of Him.

When Nicodemus found out about the clandestine, illegal meeting, it was too late to stop them. The members of the Sanhedrin were already on the way to get Pilate to order Jesus' execution. Nicodemus said that when Pilate discovered that Jesus was a Galilean, he told them to take Him before King Herod, who was in Jerusalem for the Passover, so they did. Herod refused to find fault with Him, so they took Him back to Pilate and charged Him with insurrection. This charge was accepted when Jesus did not dispute Pilate's question about His claim to be a king. The priests had left Pilate no escape from this action. Although Pilate is anything but a benevolent governor, he did not seem to want Jesus' blood on his hands. But if he did not sentence Him to death, his own future was at stake, because he could be declared a traitor to Rome. So the priests accomplished their goal – they are now rid of Jesus."

"Why did they want to get rid of Him? He taught love and obeying the Law which we were taught in synagogue school?" Mark asked.

"That is true, but He also taught that no man could obey the Law fully and was, therefore, guilty of sinning."

"Is that true?"

"Yes, the Law says that if you have broken even one Law, you are guilty of breaking all of them. The Pharisees, particularly, think that they are obeying all the laws and resented Jesus telling them that they are sinners. They don't want to be confronted with their lapses and Jesus pointed out these flaws in public." She paused. "He was drawing many followers, so they were jealous, too. I guess these things brought those Jesus' teachings offended together in the desire to remove Him."

Mark was left kneeling next to her chair in silent disbelief as his mother rose and went to the privacy of her room. They did not go out of the house on the Sabbath. Both of them remained in seclusion that day, pondering the terrible event. Sabbath had ended with sundown, but it was later that evening when the housekeeper gently knocked on the door to Mary's room. Mark heard their hushed voices followed by his mother's quickened steps.

He left his room and followed, stopping at the top of the stairs. Below, he saw Mary of Magdala speaking with her. When they parted, his mother turned to the kitchen. Mark sat down on the step to think. He was still there when Mary Magdalene returned accompanied by Salome, Joanna and another Mary, their arms full of bundles. The women went to the kitchen. When Mark entered the room, he found them busily working.

"What are you doing?" he asked. His mother looked up at him and smiled a sad smile as she replied,

"We are preparing spices to take in the morning to the tomb where they have laid Jesus' body – the last act of service we can do for Him."

Mark marveled at his mother as he returned to his room. *She is always doing things for people – even in times like this. Perhaps there was something that I can do for Jesus, too.*

He returned to his bed and fell asleep thinking on this. *If even the priests can't live without sinning, how can I? Maybe if I try to remember all that Jesus said I should do, I will learn to live a godly life. Maybe if I write down all that I remember, I will remember more. Maybe I could see if I could follow Peter, the leader of the disciples, and learn more from him. Surely Mother will allow me to do this. Then I could honor Jesus by living the way He wants me to live and serve His heavenly Father. I will start today, but I must wait for an opportune time to approach Mother about leaving to go with Peter. I pray God will help her to see my plan and show me the right time.*

James, the Brother of Jesus

1 John 2:10
Whoever loves his brother abides in the light, and in him there is no cause for stumbling.

James hadn't been there when his brother died on the cross. *I told Jesus so many times that He was making the wrong people angry with Him, but as usual Jesus hadn't listened to anything I said. Now He has reaped the consequences for His actions! He should have listened to my warnings. I was the faithful son who provided for the family after He left to go on this fool's mission,* Jesus' younger half-brother thought.

Even as a child, it bothered me the way He seemed to be preferred above all of Father's other children. Father listened with rapt attention when Jesus spoke and never punished Him — but Jesus never did anything that deserved correction. The other children and I always received retribution for our misdeeds. And that wasn't all!

Our father's position hadn't seemed natural to me when we were growing up. It was almost like Father felt inferior to his oldest child! I resented Jesus, even though He treated me well. He never talked down to me or admonished me for anything I did or didn't do. He never told on me when I did something wrong, the way our younger brother, Simon, always did. Jesus just looked at me with sadness on His face and that shamed me more than any words.

When Father died, Jesus was a young man and had worked in the carpenter shop with Father since his bar mitzvah. Both Father and Jesus had a reputation as fine carpenters. There was always ample work so all the younger brothers apprenticed in the trade as well. At Father's death, Jesus wept for him and mourned for several days. Then He went back to the carpentry work Father had taught to Him so well. The work kept all of us busy for several years and we all became skilled craftsmen.

Then one day, Jesus told Mother that He was leaving. He said that it was time He should go about His Father's business. No one but Mother completely understood what He meant. Wasn't his father's business the carpentry shop? And to add to our confusion, Mother constantly tried to get us to believe that Jesus was meant to be a rabbi – God's will, she said. Receiving her blessing, Jesus left me to head up the family. I was old enough at twenty-seven, but I wanted to get married and didn't want to be saddled with caring for my father's family. Why, had Mother given her blessing to this irresponsible son? Why didn't she hold Him responsible as the eldest son for the expected familial duties?

The first time Jesus left Nazareth He was gone for several months and when He did come back, He had followers with him. These men were nothing but common fishermen, except for one tax collector and a zealot. Most of them were distantly related to our family, but then, nearly everyone in Galilee was related in some way or another.

An angry James saw his brother as the leader of a band of ne'er-do-wells who were living off the land and the people who worked it. However, there was one event that caused him to wonder who his brother really was.

The family was invited to a wedding in nearby Cana, so Mary, James and the whole family, including Jesus and His followers went to it. Everyone was in a festive spirit as they walked along the road.

When they arrived at the home of the bride, Hannah, they found that the groom, Gideon, had not yet arrived to begin the wedding celebration. Hannah was completing her preparations and the girls and women went to put on their own wedding garments, leaving the men to get reacquainted with each other as they donned their wedding garments.

The sounds of revelry preceded the arrival of the bridegroom and his entourage shortly after the setting of the sun. With great joy, Hannah's parents presented her to Gideon. The pair joined hands and they all began to walk toward Gideon's new home, accompanied by the friends of the bridegroom, carrying torches to light the way and followed by the rest of the family, friends of the bride and musicians. The girls carried lit oil lamps. The company danced and everyone sang jubilant songs as they went.

James saw his Brother and the rest of His disciples singing with the other men. *Some rabbi,* he thought. *I have never seen any other rabbi having such a good time. He is walking alongside Mother and singing heartily. And she is actually condoning his conduct!* James just couldn't accept it. *Look at Him, smiling at everyone. Rabbis should be somber and thoughtful*, he reflected, *not laughing and joking with their followers. Theirs is a solemn message from God. They should maintain a serious demeanor at all times,* he groused to himself as they walked through the moonlit town.

The groom's house was awash in light, readily seen from a distance. The celebration was mounting with every step. Only those with torches and lamps resisted the revelers' antics. Inside the courtyard, a large number of servants quickly washed the guests' feet. Jars of fragrant oil were provided on nearby tables for anointing the guests. The governor of the feast had carefully attended to all of the amenities. There were tables heavily laden with baskets and bowls filled with all kinds of food – dates, almonds, pomegranates, apricots, lamb, veal, figs, apples, vegetables, breads, jars of honey and much more. It wasn't long before an abundant supply of wine further enlivened the festivities. After the troth was pledged by bride and bridegroom and the supper consumed, everyone broke into dancing and singing and more wine drinking.

As the festivities mounted, one of the servants advised the head servant that there was no more wine. The man went to the storeroom. Mary overheard what was said and immediately went looking for Jesus. James saw and followed her.

"They have no wine." she said, when she found Jesus.

"Woman, what does this have to do with me?" He asked. "My hour has not yet come." James was dumbfounded for he had never heard Jesus speak to their mother in such a voice of authority.

Taking Him by the hand, Mary led Jesus to the storeroom. The head servant was contemplating his dilemma. He would not be able to replenish the supply until morning and how would the revelers react to this situation? He shuddered at the thought.

"Do whatever he tells you." Mary said, pointing her finger at the servants. Then she left, brushing past the watching James. Jesus quickly looked around the room and saw six very large stone waterpots, which had been used to supply water for the foot-washing earlier.

"Fill the jars with water," He instructed and the servants did as He said, filling them to the brim. "Now draw some out and take it to the master of the feast," He told them as He walked out of the room.

The servants looked at one another. *Do we dare to take water to the governor?* But they did as Jesus had said. Drawing out a cupful, the head servant hastened to find the governor of the feast and gave him the cup. Upon tasting it, the man went to find the bridegroom. James followed him and watched with amazement as the bridegroom drank. He smacked his lips. He didn't know where the servants had found this wine, but he knew that it was of excellent quality.

"Everyone serves the good wine first," the master of the feast said to the bridegroom, "and when people have drunk freely, then the poor wine. But you have kept the good wine until now." Neither the bridegroom nor the governor knew where the wine had come from, and that set James to thinking.

Did Jesus have anything to do with it? Had He magically changed water into wine? Did Mother know that Jesus could do such a thing? He asked his mother about it later, but all she gave him was the same answer she had given all along, which he couldn't accept.

With great reluctance, James assumed the role of head of the household, but when his mother frequently went to hear Jesus preach at nearby villages, James fumed. Their neighbors whispered about Jesus. They were sure that Jesus was not right in His mind. It embarrassed James and his brothers and sisters.

He still chafed when he remembered the Sabbath Jesus had come to Nazareth and preached at the synagogue. He was handed the scroll of the prophet Isaiah and read "The Spirit of the Lord is upon me, because he has anointed me to proclaim good news to the poor. He has sent me to proclaim liberty to the captives and recovering of sight to the blind, to set at liberty those who are oppressed, to proclaim the year of the Lord's favor." When Jesus finished reading the Scripture he handed the scroll to the priest and James couldn't believe his ears when He turned to the congregation and said, "Today this Scripture has been fulfilled in your hearing."

James saw the men in the congregation turn to one another, marveling at the words Jesus said. Several times he heard someone say, "Is not this Joseph's son?" *Perhaps Jesus is a prophet of God,* he thought. He smiled at the man sitting next to him and received an approving nod back from him. Jesus continued,

"Doubtless, you will quote to me this proverb, 'Physician, heal yourself.' What we have heard you did at Capernaum, do here in your hometown as well. Truly, I say to you, no prophet is acceptable in his hometown. But in truth, I tell you, there were many widows in Israel in the days of Elijah, when the the heavens were shut up three years and six months, and a great famine came over all the land, and Elijah was sent to none of them but only to Zarephath, in the land of Sidon, to a woman who was a widow. And there were many lepers in Israel in the time of the prophet Elisha, and none of them was cleansed, but only Naaman the Syrian." The assembly fell into a stunned silence as Jesus continued to speak. Then the people's mood changed. They began saying among themselves,

"This is not right!"

"Where does this man get this wisdom and mighty works?"

"Isn't this the carpenter's son?"

"Is not his mother called Mary?"

"And His brothers James, Joses, Simon and Judas?"

"And His sisters, are they not with us?"

"Where did this man get all these things?"

"This is not what he learned in the synagogue."

"He is blaspheming!"

Suddenly one man grabbed Jesus by the arm and several others rushed forward. James retreated into the shadows away from the suddenly surly crowd. The ranting, angry mob was leading Jesus out of the synagogue, moving as one as they took his Brother to the brow of the hill outside Nazareth. *They intend to throw Him off the cliff to His death! I can't let that happen!* James realized. He left his refuge and hastened to follow them out of the village. When the front of the mob reached the top of the hill, they bunched up, chanting "No more lies! No more lies!"

As he caught up with the crowd, James was astonished to see Jesus calmly walking out from their midst. Upon reaching the edge of the mob, Jesus strode down the hill and out of sight, unnoticed by them. The leaders of the group were still standing at the brow, arguing, completely oblivious to the fact that the object of their anger was no longer there.

James didn't say anything about the event to Mary then, but she heard about it from someone else and asked him why he hadn't stopped it from happening. James answered, "Am I my brother's keeper?"

At first there had been whispers among the villagers about Joseph's "mad" son, which grew in both frequency and volume. Soon, James, his siblings and their mother were continually suffering derision. His sisters, Salome and Anne, refused to go to the well for water, so Mary asked Simon to get the family's supply. All the women stayed close to the house unless one of the men was with them.

Then one day word came that Jesus had come to Cana, a nearby town, and was preaching there.

"Mother, my brothers and I will go and tell Him to stop this foolishness," James said.

"I must go, too," Mary replied. "He may not listen to you, but He has always listened to me."

"Perhaps you are right," James agreed and the five of them set off for Cana, where they found Jesus teaching in the synagogue. The place was so crowded that the people who couldn't get in were standing as near the door as possible in order to hear. James pushed his way to the man attending the door and asked him to tell Jesus that His mother and brothers were here and needed to speak with Him. After a long time, the man returned, saying that Jesus had heard the message, then they heard Jesus say to the crowd of people inside,

"Who is my mother, and who are my brothers? Here are my mother and my brothers! For whoever does the will of my Father in heaven is my brother and sister and mother."

James, Mary and the rest of the family were shocked. It was a sad trip home. James decided that he would never again try to convince Jesus of His first obligation to His family. But Mary understood that Jesus was fulfilling His first obligation to God, as He had been destined to do since that night when the messenger of God had told her that she was to be the earthly mother of His Son!

And now, Jesus had thrown the last stone right at James' heart. He had been furious when his friend, Eli, had told him what he heard Jesus say from the cross.

"Woman, behold your son." And to His follower, John, who was supporting Mary as they stood together before the cross of suffering, watching Him die, He said, "Behold your mother."

Jesus gave my mother into the care of that foolish young boy who has been following Him these past three years! Did He forget that I am the one who has cared for her since the day He left home on this folly of His? I am certainly capable of caring for my own mother better than a stranger! I must get this straightened out! I broke Sabbath to get here, but the matter must be settled — and settled now!

His fist struck mighty blows on the door of John's quarters. Behind the door he could hear the weeping of a woman. John opened the door and James pushed him aside, following the sound of sobbing to the room where Mary lay on the bed facing the wall.

"I've come for you, Mother," he said. Mary rolled onto her back and looked up at him. There was no sign of recognition on her face. She turned her head back toward the wall. James spun around and faced John, who had followed him into the room.

"What have you done to her?" James demanded.

"Comforted her and cared for her," John answered, "as the Lord commanded me to do."

"Jesus didn't know what He was saying," James yelled.

"Please come into the other room and we'll discuss it," John replied calmly.

"No, she is my mother and I want her to come home with me right now. I'll care for her. We don't need you." Mary turned back, raised up on her elbow and touched James' arm.

"Please," she said in a thin voice, "do not be angry with John. He is only doing as Jesus told him to do. He is caring for me well."

"And I will continue to do so until the end of life," John added.

"But he is not your son," James pleaded. "I am! You belong with your family. Come with me and let your children care for you."

"No, my son," Mary answered firmly. "Jesus knows what is best. You will have important work to do, too. Please, accept this. It is my desire to stay with John. May God bless you, son."

She laid her head down and turned again to the wall. James knelt beside the bed and tenderly put his hand on her shoulder. Mary closed her eyes and did not move.

"Mother," James cried in anguish, "what is wrong with me? Am I not fit to care for you? Don't you like your life in

Nazareth? What does this fellow mean to you? Please come home to your family. That's where you belong. We want you to be with us." His head rested on her arm, but she did not respond. He shook her, but John stepped forward and pulled his hands away.

James rose and turned on him, fire shooting from his eyes as they met John's. For a long moment the two men stood facing each other, neither saying a word. James looked down again at his mother. She did not even look his direction. Then he pushed John aside and stormed out. *I am totally confused, but it will do no good to say more now. Her refusal to come speaks louder than any explanation she could give. What did she mean when she said that I would have work to do? Carpentry work is all that awaits me. She knows that I could easily care for her and keep the shop working. Maybe she meant that I will be saddled with caring for the family until both of my sisters are married. That could be years! There is only one thing left for me to do, I'll leave Jerusalem in the morning, but perhaps I will try one more time to convince Mother to come home with me. I'll think about it tonight.*

Pulling his mantle close in the chill night air, his dark rage showed in his sparking eyes as he stomped down the street to the place he was staying during Passover. His countenance glowered as he gained resolve. *She will have to listen to me tomorrow. She* will *come home with me. She will!*

Part II
Day of Light

John 1:3- 5
All things were made through him, and without
him was not anything made that was made.
In him was life, and the life was the light of men.
The light shines in the darkness,
and the darkness has not overcome it.

Dawn

James 1:17
Every good gift and every perfect gift is from above, coming down from the Father of lights with whom there is no variation or shadow due to change.

"I wonder how long we will be on this duty," grumbled the Roman soldier as he threw another piece of wood on the fire.

"Not much longer now," answered the captain. He, too, resented the reason they were spending three days in this garden cemetery.

"Why are we here at all?" asked another impatient soldier.

"It was those infernal priests demanding that Pilate post a guard on a dead man's tomb. They said the man had claimed that if he was killed, he would come back to life in three days," said the captain, "and they didn't want his followers to steal his body and claim that he had risen from the dead."

"So," scoffed another man, "we are to stand here in this dewy morning to make sure that they can't steal a body? I say, let them have it!"

"There will be no desertion of this post while I am

in charge," stated the captain as he pulled his cloak tighter around him and leaned back against a gnarled olive tree trunk.

He was looking at the stone rolled against the tomb's opening. *It would take several men to move that stone,* he thought. *Perhaps I had better increase the watch and assign two men to stand guard at the same time. If there is to be an attempt to steal the body, one man might be overpowered before he could give alarm, but two ought to prevent that. If they attempt to act in three days, this would have to be the time.*

"You, there," the captain barked, gesturing to one of those sitting near the fire, "stand guard with him." The soldier obeyed, but threw a menacing look at the captain.

It was still dark when Mary Magdalene lightly rapped on the entrance door. Mary, John Mark's mother, answered it. She was carrying a small oil lamp to light the way through the darkened house to the kitchen. Salome, Joanna and the other Mary had just finished assembling the bundles filled with spices which they would carry to the tomb this morning. Each woman carefully picked up a bundle and placed it on her head. Quietly, they left the house.

The streets were still dark and in several places, one of the women stumbled on a protruding stone, but her companions caught her arms and kept her from falling or losing her bundle. Gradually they made their way to the city gate through which, only three days earlier, their Savior was taken to Golgotha, the place of the skull, where He had died.

Mary Magdalene knew where her Lord was buried as she had followed the men who removed Jesus' body from the cross that terrible day. Mary had seen the tomb where they laid Him, but she had not tarried there lest someone become suspicious and arrest her.

Silently, she led the women through Jerusalem's quiet streets. Before the sun's first rays were beginning to peek over the Mount of Olives they were at the city gate. They were allowed to go through the pedestrian door for the gate was not yet opened for traffic.

Removing the bundles from their heads so they could pass through the low door, each one handed her bundle to one of the others, went to the other side of the massive gate, then received it back. When they were all on the Damascus Road side of the gate, they put the bundles back in place on the top of their heads and resumed their walk. The tomb was not far from there and they hurried to reach it before the sun filled the valley. Joanna, touched Mary's shoulder and whispered to her.

"How will we roll the stone from the tomb?" she asked.

"You said that it was very big," added Salome.

"Yes," Mary answered, "it is very big and will be very heavy."

"Perhaps the soldiers will help us," offered the other Mary.

Mary Magdalene saw the guard by the tomb and signaled her companions to stop where they were still hidden by the trees of the garden from the soldier's view. She laid down her bundle. She was going on ahead alone to see what the situation was. She had walked only a few feet toward the tomb when the earth began to shake.

"This cursed country," exploded one of the men, "I'll never get used to it shaking."

The next instant the early morning darkness of the valley was rent by a brilliant light. All of the soldiers were paralyzed with fear and neither spoke nor moved as they heard the rumble and watched the enormous stone being rolled away from the opening of the tomb. They saw not a single person! Then as abruptly as it had come, the light was gone and the darkness was broken only by the campfire with which the guards had warmed themselves.

When they regained their senses, the captain looked at his men. No one spoke, but they looked at each other, silently asking *"Did you see that? What was it?"* Everything was still. They had heard no running feet – had seen no one but themselves. Turning to his men, he asked,

"What did you see?"

"We saw nothing," the soldiers answered him as one. The captain looked again at the gaping entrance to the tomb. Reaching down, he picked up a brand from the fire to use as a torch and walked to the entrance of the tomb.

Cautiously, he peered in. He saw a partially completed bed on the right side of the tomb, but on the left, on the bed where the body had been laid, only the grave clothes remained. Looking more closely, he saw something strange. The napkin which had been used to cover the corpse's head, was neatly folded and laid on the stone pillow. The shroud was still in place, but empty! It looked like the dead man had awakened, slipped out of the grave clothes, folded the napkin and walked out. *But if indeed this had happened, how could he have moved the enormous stone – from inside the tomb – alone?*

"Come," ordered the returning captain as he threw the brand back on the fire, "we will go tell the priests what has happened." Immediately they formed up, marched past the place where the small group of women were standing behind some trees a little way from the path and continued through the now opened city gate, making haste to the Temple.

The women shrank back farther from the pathway while the troops passed, then carefully ventured forward. Mary Magdalene picked up her bundle of spices and placed it on her head. The others followed her lead.

Cautiously, a few steps at a time, the little group advanced toward the crypt. When they reached the dying campfire, they clearly saw the entrance to the tomb. It was open! The stone had been rolled away!

One by one, they laid down their bundles near the campfire. As they curiously peered through the gaping doorway in dawn's dim first light, they saw a young man sitting on the right side of the chamber opposite the bed on which Jesus' body had been placed. They stared at him and he spoke.

"Do not be alarmed. You seek Jesus of Nazareth, who was crucified. He is risen! He is not here! See the place where they laid Him. But go and tell His disciples – and Peter – that He is going before you into Galilee; there you will see Him as He said to you."

Startled and afraid, the women turned and looked quickly at the place indicated by the young man. Seeing that it held only the empty grave clothes, they ran panic-stricken out of the entrance and back to Jerusalem.

All of them ran except Mary Magdalene who stopped next to the soldier's campfire and turned back. She was standing alone in the garden near her companions abandoned bundles, but her eyes were transfixed on the gaping entrance. Tears welled up and she sank to her knees. It was still so unbelievable to her that she would never see Him again. Or hear his musical voice. Or learn more of His wisdom. She was unable to contain her grief any longer. She bowed her head and wept in a sorrow, heightened by not being able to perform her last act of love.

"Woman, why are you weeping? Whom are you seeking?" came the soft voice. Opening her eyes, Mary realized that she was not alone – there were a man's feet standing next to her. Supposing him to be the gardener, with her eyes still lowered, she replied, "Because they have taken away my Lord, and I do not know where they have laid Him. Sir, if You have carried Him away, tell me where You have laid Him, and I will take Him away."

"Mary," the voice said. It sounded so tender – so familiar. Still kneeling, she slowly raised her eyes. When her gaze found the speaker's face, she could hardly believe who she saw. She was amazed – overjoyed – as the first light of recognition revealed that Jesus had addressed her.

"Rabboni!" she exclaimed as she stretched out her arms to embrace His feet. "Do not cling to Me. I have not yet ascended to My Father. Go to My brethren and say to them, 'I am ascending to My Father and your Father, and to My God and your God'," He instructed and then He was gone.

Mary looked all about her, but she didn't see anyone anywhere. She slowly arose and looked around again. *Could it really be true? My Savior is alive! He spoke to me! Although I can't see Him, I still feel His presence and know that I have not been deceived. I must hurry to tell the others.* Filled with inexpressible joy, leaving behind the bundles of spice, she ran from the garden, through the city gates, down the streets until she arrived at Mary's house.

Meanwhile, the captain and his men arrived at the Temple. Boldly, they entered the outer courtyard and marched toward the Temple itself. Immediately, two priests approached them.

"Hold up there," one of them said to the Romans, "Only Jews may enter the Temple."

"I am aware of that, sir," replied the captain, "but I must speak with the High Priest on a matter of greatest urgency."

"Perhaps we can help you," offered the other priest.

"I said that I need to speak with the High Priest and to

him only," the captain repeated emphatically.

"Wait here and I will see if he is ready to receive visitors," the first priest stated.

"I am not under his command," the captain barked.

"Yes, sir," the other priest said, tugging his companion's sleeve, "we will tell him of the urgency. Please wait in this room."

Having thus deposited the Romans in an anteroom, the two priests went up the stairs to the chief priest's chamber.

"My lord," the first priest softly said at the door to his room, "there are some Roman soldiers asking for you."

"What do they want?" came an angry burst of words. "They should not be in the Temple."

"They are waiting for you in the anteroom, my lord," the priest replied.

"Tell them that I will be with them presently."

"My lord, the captain said that the matter was very urgent."

"Tell him that I will be with him presently. Send messengers out to all the elders, and instruct them to come immediately to the Temple. Go!"

The second priest returned to the anteroom and delivered the High Priest Caiaphas' message to the Romans.

"Didn't he understand that this is of the utmost urgency?" the captain cried out in frustration. "It affects him directly."

"I have told you his reply, now I must attend to my duties. You will continue to wait here for the High Priest."

The captain looked at his command as the priest walked away. He felt like a trapped animal. He shrugged his shoulders as he walked to a wall and leaned against it for support. He hated the arrogance of the Jewish Sanhedrin and that air of superiority was particularly strong in this chief priest, but he and his men were now firmly in a trap of his own making.

Perhaps my decision to come to the Temple instead of to our superior had been the wrong one after all. Maybe I should have faced the commander with our failure to protect the body in the tomb as I was ordered, but I know that that action would have certainly resulted in the executions of all of us. I thought instead there was a slim possibility that by coming first to the Jewish priest who had insisted on the guard and telling him of the morning's events, we might gain a reprieve from that certain death.

The captain was aware that some intrigue was involved in the office of the High Priest. He knew little of Caiaphas' rise to the position, but he was certain that it had something to do with his father-in-law, Ananias, the former chief priest. Although he was no longer an official, the former high priest still controlled most of what went on in Jerusalem, and thereby in the whole of Israel. When he left office after serving nine years, he appointed a succession of three other relatives as High Priest, but the Romans found none of them satisfactory. When Ananias appointed Caiaphas, the Romans found what they were looking for – one who would properly submit to all they decreed for the Jewish people and would enforce it with his own temple guard.

By the time Caiaphas finally summoned the waiting Romans to a large meeting room, they were in a state of high anxiety, but they tried to hide their emotions behind military demeanor. As they entered the room, they saw a group of twenty to twenty-five Jews seated on the bench around the wall. The soldiers stiffened. They tried not to let the fear that was in their hearts show on their faces. It appeared that they were to be tried by these haughty Jews and they could not imagine what to expect.

"Why did you come here, captain?" demanded Caiaphas.

"Sir, we have come to bring you some urgent news," the captain began.

"Why did you come here, instead of to your commander?" Caiaphas interrupted.

"Sir, we came to you because we thought that you needed to know what happened before anyone else."

"And what did happen?"

"We were at the tomb as ordered. Two men were standing guard, one on each side of the stone across the entrance. The rest of us were talking around the campfire about ten feet away. Nothing unusual had happened all night nor during the previous night and the vigil was to last only a few hours longer, when the earth began to shake. Then there was a brilliant light. I tried to move, but couldn't. It was like I was paralyzed. As we watched, it appeared that the stone rolled away from the entrance by itself. Then the light was gone and we were able to move. Indeed the stone had been rolled away from the door of the tomb. None of us saw or heard anything but the light and the movement of the stone.

"When the light was gone and I could move again, I picked up a brand from the fire and went to look in the tomb. There was no body there – only the grave clothes lying on the bed. So far as we know, there was no one else there. None of us saw anyone. We heard no one running away. We do not know what happened, but I swear that is the whole story, sir," the captain ended.

"Thank you, Captain," Caiaphas said, turning to the other soldiers, "Did any of you see something else?"

The men all shook their heads. "The captain has told it all," one of them said.

"And what do you want from us?" Caiaphas asked, turning again to the captain.

"How do you want us to handle this situation?" the captain asked in reply. "Should we report this event to our superior?"

"You will wait in the anteroom while we deliberate," Caiaphas instructed and turned away from them.

"What is going to happen to us, Captain?" asked one of the men when the door to the anteroom closed.

"I don't know, but we could still pay with our lives for the failure of our mission," he replied.

"Was it really wise to come here rather than to our superior, Captain?" asked another.

"At the time I made the decision, it seemed right. We'll see," he answered.

It was nearly an hour before they were summoned back to the chamber. Standing uneasily at attention before these Jews, the Roman soldiers awaited their decision, expecting the sentence of death. Instead they were amazed at what they heard.

"You and your men did well to come to us first," Caiaphas, the High Priest, began. "Here's what you will do – report back to your commander as if nothing happened and to everyone, report that 'His disciples came at night and stole Him away while we slept.' If this comes to the governor's ears, we will appease him and make you secure. In appreciation for your cooperation in this matter, we are giving you a gift which you may share with your men," he said as he handed the captain a bag containing a large sum of money.

The captain looked closely into the High Priest's eyes as he took the bag. *Is he paying for our silence? I do not see any*

132

sign of deceit in the man's gaze, so the captain nodded his agreement and he and his men left the chamber and the Temple. The time for them to report back to the Antonio Fortress was approaching as they huddled together in an alley and the captain counted out to each man his share of the sum. Quietly, one by one, they took a solemn oath to tell no one the truth – ever.

Peter and John had just arrived at Mary's house when the women rushed in and told them about their encounter with the young man at the tomb. Peter was skeptical and dismissed the whole story as the women's hysteria, but John was captured by the thought and as he pondered it, memories of some of Jesus' words began to come back to him.

By the time Mary Magdalene reached Mary's house, she could contain herself no longer. Without waiting for the door to be answered, she burst into the room.

"He is alive!" she shouted above the raised voices of those present, "He is alive! He is alive! He is alive!"

"Who?" demanded an astonished Peter.

"How do you know?" John asked.

"This is what we have been trying to tell them, but they don't believe us," cried Salome, looking to Mary Magdalene for confirmation.

"It is true!" Mary shouted above the din, "I have seen Him and He spoke to me! He is alive! Where is His mother? I must tell her the good news!"

"She is still resting in my quarters," John replied, "but first tell us more. Where did you see Him? How do you know that you really saw the Master?"

"When the others fled from the empty tomb, I couldn't. I just knelt there and cried out to the Lord," she told them. "Suddenly I realized that there was a man standing beside me.

Without looking up, I thought that he was the gardener and would know where they had taken Jesus. I pleaded with him to tell me, but when he said, 'Mary' I knew that was the voice of my Lord!"

John looked at Peter and exclaimed, "I must go and see for myself." He darted out the door. Peter was close on his heels as they ran down the streets and through the city gates, but the younger John outdistanced him. By the time Peter caught up with him, John was standing inside the entrance of the tomb, dumbfounded by what he saw. On the bed where Jesus' body had been placed were the grave clothes with the napkin that covered His face, neatly folded and laying on the stone pillow. *Jesus' body had not been crudely dragged away! It was as if He sat up and carefully folded the head cloth, placing it where it now lay! Did He truly awaken from death? Where is He now? If He truly is alive, we will see Him again!* Their hearts were racing.

Both men stood there in stunned silence as they processed what they saw and the first light of the truth Jesus had spoken to them filled their minds and souls. *The stone had been rolled back. The tomb was open! This would have taken several men. Mary and the women had seen the blinding light, but no one but the soldiers and they had been frozen in place. The tomb was not desecrated in any way, but had been left in order. And, most importantly,* **Jesus was not there!**

They left the silent tomb in a state of wonder and returned to the disciples who were gathered at Mary's House.

Morning

Deuteronomy 4:29-30
But from there you will seek the Lord your God and you will find him, if you search after him with all your heart and with all your soul. When you are in tribulation, and all these things come upon you in the latter days, you will return to the Lord your God and obey his voice.

"Nicodemus!" Joseph of Arimathea shouted as he barged through the outer door of Nicodemus' residence, pushing aside the startled servant. "Get up! You've got to hear what has happened," he called as he climbed the stairway to his friend's bedroom and threw open the door, revealing a suddenly awakened Nicodemus just arising from bed.

"What is it?" he asked.

"Caiaphas called an emergency meeting of the elders early this morning," came the answer.

"Why would he do such a thing? How did you hear about it?" Nicodemus' questions tumbled out.

"Mattathias came to see me as soon as the meeting ended," Joseph told him. "He said that the Roman guard which had been standing watch on the tomb awakened Caiaphas and their captain told the assembly of elders that the body of Jesus has disappeared."

"His body disappeared! How?" Nicodemus exclaimed.

"Mattathias said the captain swore they were standing watch as ordered when there was an earthquake," Joseph began.

"Yes, I felt it very early this morning," Nicodemus agreed.

"The captain said that it was as if they were frozen in place and could not move," Joseph continued. "Then the stone was rolled back from the entrance. A blinding light blazed for a moment and then everything was suddenly just as it was. The captain said that when he recovered his senses, he went to look in the now exposed tomb and there was no body in it! He wanted to know what to do, because if he went back to his superiors with this story, he and the guards would be executed for not fulfilling their duty."

"And why did Caiaphas call the meeting?"

"He and the elders had to come up with a plan to forestall the possibility that the 'myth' of Jesus would become even stronger than the man had been."

"I see," studied Nicodemus. "Do you think that maybe they believed that Jesus had come back to life as He told us all He would?"

"I think that is exactly what they fear!" Joseph answered, continuing. "A lot of suggestions were made and the one they acted on was this. They instructed the guard to tell their superiors and everyone else that the disciples stole the body from the tomb while they slept."

"Why would the soldiers do that? It would surely mean their execution!"

"Because the elders bribed them with a large bag of money and the promise that they would appease Pilate if it should come to his ears."

"So they cast the blame on the disciples as a plot to keep

themselves in power," Nicodemus pondered aloud. "Caiaphas may also send Temple Guard to arrest Jesus' followers in order to lend credence to this plan. I must go tell the followers of the treachery afoot so they can protect themselves." Reaching for his robe as he arose, he thanked Joseph for the news and went to dress.

Mary Magdalene hesitated as she raised her hand to knock on the door of John's quarters. Mary, Jesus' mother, had been staying there since the crucifixion. John had lovingly taken her home with him as Jesus had instructed and she had remained in solitude to mourn, but now Magdalene heard raised voices coming from inside the rooms. She recognized Mary's voice, but not that of the man with whom she was arguing, so she stood there for a moment, listening.

"Mother," said the man, "you must come with me now. Look how John has left you alone and gone off somewhere. He will not care for you as well as our family will. I'll get your things together and we will be off."

"No," Mary said emphatically, "I will stay with John. You were not always with me, either. You must leave – now!"

"I'll not go without you," he shouted.

Mary Magdalene knocked firmly on the door and called out, "Mary, I must talk with you at once. May I come in?"

"Please come in," Mary responded. Mary Magdalene opened the door and saw James, the brother of Jesus, holding onto his mother's arm.

"Is there anything I can do to help?" she asked.

"Stay out of this," James growled, "it is a matter between my mother and me."

"Was there something you needed?" asked Mary as she jerked her arm free.

"I have wonderful news and I wanted to share it with you immediately," the Magdalene answered.

"What can be so wonderful?" snapped James. "My brother is dead and you fools are partly to blame! You followed Him and encouraged Him in His folly. How could anything having to do with you be wonderful?"

"Mary," came the soft joyous answer, "Your Son is not dead! He is alive and I have seen Him and spoken to Him. He is alive! Raised from the dead! Alive!"

"Nonsense," scoffed James. "The Romans are thorough butchers."

"It is true! He is alive!" Mary Magdalene repeated.

Jesus' mother sank to her knees with her head bowed as the first light of the fulfillment of the angel's message flooded her being.

"Thank you, Father, for raising Your Son. Everything that Your angel told me so long ago has come to pass. Now the world will know Him as we know Him – as Your one true Son. Blessed be Your name, O God."

"Where do you claim you saw Jesus alive?" James demanded.

"In the garden near the tomb where He was laid."

"Come and show us," James hurled as he reached for his mother's arm and drew her to her feet. "I don't believe any of this. We'll see if you are telling a cruel lie." He strode toward the door dragging his mother with him.

Mary Magdalene looked in disbelief at his harsh, unsympathetic actions. Then she walked over to him and took hold of his arm. She looked straight into his eyes.

"I am telling the truth," she said, as she loosed his grip on Mary's arm, adding, "It is not right that you drag your mother along, but come by yourself and I will show you the empty tomb. If she wants to come, she will do it on her own."

Suddenly the figure of John filled the door. Surveying the scene, he approached James.

"What are you doing here, James?" he asked. "I told you last evening that I was taking care of your mother from now on. Please go and do not bother her, again."

"I suppose that you believe that Jesus is alive, too," James sneered at him.

"I know that He is!" John replied. Mary gasped at John's affirmation.

"Then *you* show me the proof," James demanded.

"I'll be pleased to do so, but your mother should go with Mary to the place the disciples are gathered," John said. He stepped aside as James released his mother's arm and defiantly strode out the door.

When the men had gone down the street toward the city gates, the two women closed the door to the rooms behind them and went to meet the others, both faces aglow with joy.

Mary's house was buzzing with excited voices as those who had visited the tomb that morning, compared notes and relived their discovery with the others. The house was growing very crowded as more and more followers arrived. Those who had fled to Bethany the night of the arrest had been among the first ones to arrive that morning. They had anxiously awaited the opening of the city gates, but the heavy traffic as vendors converged for market day had impeded their progress. Finally, the journey through the twisting, narrow, congested streets brought the men to Mary's house. Their knock on the door was answered by John Mark, Mary's son. and the disciples came in.

"We heard that Jesus was crucified on Friday. Where have they laid His body?" Matthew asked him.

"Two Pharisees took it down from the cross," Mark told them.

"What more could they do to Him? Wasn't it enough that they killed Him?" demanded Simon the Zealot.

"The two Pharisees were Nicodemus and Joseph of Arimathia and they took His body to Joseph's new tomb to properly bury Him," Mark explained.

"They buried Him in a Pharisee's tomb?"

"Yes," Mark answered.

"Why?"

"We think they secretly believed that Jesus was Messiah."

"Where is Peter?" Andrew asked Mark.

"He and John have gone to the tomb."

"Where is the tomb? We will go there to honor Him, too," demanded Simon the Zealot.

"Near Golgotha," came the answer, "but Jesus is not there."

"Not there?!"

"No, Peter and John have gone to see."

"See what?"

"Mary Magdalene said that He is risen and she has spoken with Him." The disciples stood there with their mouths open. *Could Jesus really be alive?*

"Where?" asked Philip.

"In the garden by the tomb."

"Where is Mary?" Matthew asked. "We must see her."

"Here I am," said Mary as she and Jesus' mother walked through the open door. "It is true! He is alive! God raised Him from the dead and He spoke to me this morning."

"Woman, are you sure? Was it really Jesus?" asked Philip.

"Yes, I am sure," she affirmed, "He told me to come and tell the brothers and Peter to go to Galilee and He would see you there."

"I can't believe it!" gasped Thomas as the group received the first light of truth.

During this exchange, other followers arrived, including a couple from Emmaus. Clopas, a cousin of Salome, and his wife, Mary, had been greatly distressed when they heard of Jesus' death. They had listened to Jesus speak many times and placed their faith in His claim to be Messiah. They came to learn if the stories they had heard of His crucifixion were true. And if they were true, did anyone know if God would avenge His Son's death? Intently they listened to the conversation. They were confused. *How could God's Son die? Did He die? What will happen to those of us who followed Him now?*

Suddenly, the entrance door burst open again. Nicodemus stood there, his cloak in disarray from his desperate journey through the crowded streets.

"I bring distressing news," he exclaimed. "The priests are claiming that you have stolen Jesus' body! They may be sending soldiers to arrest you as we speak!"

"Arrest us? For stealing the Lord's body?" Andrew gasped.

"Did *you* steal it?" one of the men demanded of the women.

"No," Mary Magdalene affirmed in a steely voice.

"Then who did?" asked another.

Peter stepped forward, having just arrived back from the tomb. He raised his hand to still the noise, before he addressed them. "We do not know who stole the body – if, indeed, it has been stolen," he said.

"What do you mean by that?" came a harsh retort.

"When John and I saw the tomb this morning, it didn't have the appearance of someone carelessly or hurriedly snatching our Lord's body and carrying it away. Instead, it looked as if He got up, carefully folded the napkin that covered His face and laid it on the pillow. The grave clothes were still in place. In other words, the tomb did not look as if it had been violated as it would have been during a theft."

"How can that be?" asked Nicodemus. "Joseph and I were witnesses to His death. Pilate even sent a soldier to ascertain that He was dead. We took His body from the cross of crucifixion. We dressed it with spices ourselves and we know that He was dead. He had already stiffened. What you are saying doesn't make sense."

"We agree," answered Peter. At that moment, John and James, Jesus' brother, entered the room. Hearing the end of the discussion, James spoke.

"No, it doesn't make sense! Yet I have seen it for myself. He is not there and the tomb was just as Peter described it. Now, I finally believe that Jesus was more than my brother, He is the true Messiah. On the way back here from the tomb, John told me some of the things he remembered Jesus saying the night of His arrest. John said he remembered that at the Passover meal, Jesus had said, 'All of you will be made to stumble because of Me this night.'

"I never understood what my mother told us about Jesus from the time we were children," James looked at his sobbing mother, who had sunk to her knees next to Mary Magdalene. He went to her side and continued, "She told us many times that Jesus was special, but we were all jealous of the way He was treated. He never did anything to deserve punishment. He was the perfect son – always obedient and helpful. He was eager to learn all that our father taught Him. He was patient as He taught us the fine points of carpentry.

"We all thought when our father died, Jesus would be

the provider for the family. That's why I was angry when one day He suddenly left us. Mother told us that this was what He was supposed to do, but we still didn't understand.

"We were embarrassed when He turned His back on us and we resented the ridicule His actions brought to the rest of the family. When He taught in the synagogue, He so inflamed the congregation that they took Him out to the brow of the hill, intending to cast Him off. I saw Him come out of the crowd and walk away unobserved. I couldn't understand how He had done that, but I still didn't believe He was anyone special. Even this morning, I was sure that He was a deluded man who thought He was more than any man could be. How could He be God's Son? He was my brother!

"But now I have seen the empty tomb where they laid Him and I received the first light of understanding. Now I see what eluded me before – now I know without a doubt that Jesus truly is the Son of God!" James knelt beside his mother and put his arms around her shoulders. She laid her head against his chest and looked up at him.

"Now you truly believe?" she asked.

"Yes, mother," James assured her as he held her closely to him. "I now see Him as you have seen Him all along. I know that Jesus is God's Son – our Messiah."

As the two embraced each other, the assembly began to murmur among themselves. The sound got louder and louder. There were an increasing number of shouts of "Praise God!" and "Hallelujah" as the full realization of what had happened took hold. Faces which had been drawn and worried only minutes before, now shined with joy and hope.

"James, now do you know why I must live with John?" Mary asked her son.

"Yes, mother," he answered, "I now know that God

Himself ordained this moment as you were trying to tell me when you said, 'You will have important work to do.' Now I know what that work is!" Raising his hands to heaven, James cried, "Thank you, Lord, for using this poor, imperfect servant. Help me, my God!"

John helped Mary to her feet. Mary Magdalene put her arm around her and the two women left to return to John's quarters so Mary could rest and consider all that had happened.

The crowded room again became abuzz with excited voices. People began to mill around, talking to each other. There was much jostling among them.

"I am afraid that something is not right," Mary, Clopas' pregnant wife, said as she touched his arm. "I feel very bad. Can we go back to our room so that I can rest?" Without hesitation, Clopas took Mary's hand and they returned to their rented room. Tenderly Clopas helped her lie down and went outside the door to ponder the event they had just witnessed. *Had someone stolen Jesus' body? Why? Was that the end of the Messiah? Did we follow Him in faith or in futility? What does Jesus want from me now? What did I expect of Jesus?* The questions seemed endless.

Clopas stepped back into the room and saw that Mary was sleeping peacefully. He decided to go to the market and get some food so when she awoke, he would have something for her to eat. He picked up the goatskin, went to the well and filled it, then went to the baker for a loaf of bread and the fruit vendor where he bought figs, some apricots and a special treat – a pomegranate, Mary's favorite.

Everyone," said Peter to those assembled, "it might be well for us to part now and go our separate ways for a time, in case the guards should come here to arrest us. It will be better if we are harder for them to find. We eleven will remain here and pray to know God's will for us all, but the rest of you should go about your business as usual and we will meet here again tonight."

Immediately the crowd started leaving, suddenly aware of the danger they might be in if they remained there longer.

"John," asked Peter as they were walking into an inner room to pray, "What was it that James said about you remembering something Jesus said at the Passover meal?"

"I remembered," John answered, "that at the Passover meal Jesus said, 'All of you will be made to stumble because of Me this night, for it is written: "'I will strike the Shepherd, and the sheep of the flock will be scattered'. But after I have been raised, I will go before you to Galilee'."

"That's right!" Peter exclaimed. "And this morning the women said they were instructed to tell us that Jesus would meet us in Galilee. Do you remember any more, John?"

"Not at this time," John responded, "but maybe if we ask God, He will help us to remember more."

With this thought in mind, the group entered into prayer seeking God's will for them. The eleven disciples' fervent prayers for guidance and direction continued all afternoon.

They felt so unworthy to try to carry on the Master's work without Him there to instruct and encourage them, but they received answers through the remembrance of many things Jesus had told them in the past few months, the message of the young man at the tomb and their own listening hearts.

The women gathered in another room. Both groups prayed as individuals and corporately for the next few hours. As the afternoon passed a few other followers trickled in, joining the prayers.

Mary was awakening when Clopas returned with the food and she was grateful for her husband's thoughtfulness. Eagerly, as they ate, they discussed what had occurred that morning. When they finished, Mary looked closely at Clopas.

"Husband, I would like to go home today. I want to be in my own home tonight. Would you mind terribly if we left now?" she asked.

"I suppose that we could go now that we know for certain that Jesus was crucified, but first I want to go back to Mary's house and see if there is any more news," he answered. "I will do that while you pack our possessions."

His wife nodded in agreement and Clopas returned to the gathering place. The crowd had dispersed before Clopas arrived back at Mary's house, so he found no one in the courtyard.

"Are there any disciples still here?" he asked the servant girl who answered his knock on the door.

"Yes," she answered, "the ones who travelled with Jesus are inside in prayer."

"Where is your mistress?"

"She is in prayer with the other women."

"What are they praying for?"

"They are asking the Lord for clear direction now."

"I see," Clopas said and he turned to leave. Now he felt even more certain that the best thing for him and Mary to do was to return home. Everything he had believed in was now in disarray and he knew that he, too, needed to seek God's leading for their lives, so he returned to their room and the two set out for the safety of home.

As they walked along the tree-lined road by the river

to their home seven miles away in Emmaus, Clopas and Mary talked about the events of the day.

"Why would anyone want to steal a dead man's body?" Mary asked, adding, "They would be unclean."

"Yes, they would," Clopas agreed. "But what bothers me most is that I didn't hear of any troops trying to arrest anyone. If the authorities thought that Jesus' followers had committed a crime, why didn't they try to arrest some of us?"

"Maybe they hadn't started to do that yet – maybe they have and we just haven't heard about it yet – or maybe they are laying a trap," offered Mary. Turning to her husband, she asked, "Do you still believe that Jesus was the Messiah?"

"I want to believe it, but I don't know," he answered. "I just don't know. Maybe nobody stole His body. Maybe it is as the disciples believe – maybe He really did rise from the dead like the women said."

"I wouldn't think they could have made up something like that."

"I don't think they did. Peter went and looked, too, and he said they had told the truth."

"Do you think Mary Magdalene really spoke to Jesus?"

"As you said, why would she say it if it wasn't true."

"Do you think we will ever see Him again?" The two had been so deep in conversation they didn't realize that a stranger had caught up to them until he spoke.

"What kind of conversation is this that you have with one another as you walk and are sad?" the stranger asked.

Clopas glanced at Mary and saw that she had been startled. Turning toward the stranger, he saw an ordinary-looking man, dressed in a tunic and cloak that looked as if he had travelled a long way.

"Are You the only stranger in Jerusalem, and have You

not known the things which happened there in these days?" Clopas asked.

"What things?" he responded.

"The things concerning Jesus of Nazareth, who was a Prophet mighty in deed and word before God and all the people," Clopas answered. "The chief priests and our rulers delivered Him to be condemned to death and crucified Him. We were hoping that it was He who was going to redeem Israel. Indeed, besides all this, today is the third day since these things happened."

"Yes," said Mary, "and certain women of our company, who arrived at the tomb early, astonished us."

"When they did not find His body, they came saying that they had also seen a vision of angels who said He was alive," stated Clopas.

"And certain of those who were with us went to the tomb and found it just as the women had said," Mary added.

"But Him they did not see," concluded Clopas.

"O foolish ones, and slow of heart to believe in all that the prophets have spoken! Ought not the Christ to have suffered these things and to enter into His glory?" the stranger said with a smile. Clopas and Mary were amazed at this remark. The man started talking to them telling them all of the scripture which referred to the Messiah. The knowledge of the Scriptures this man revealed to them as they walked along kept their attention. *Surely, he is a learned teacher,* they thought, in spite of His ragged appearance. All the way to Emmaus, the three walked while the couple listened carefully to all the stranger told them. When they neared their home, the stranger bid them farewell saying that He was going farther.

"Please eat with us before You go farther," Mary invited.

"Abide with us," Clopas said, picking up Mary's plea. "It

is toward evening and the day is far spent."

"Very well, your kind invitation is accepted," he replied. As soon as they entered their house, Mary began preparing a meal. She suddenly realized that she was feeling fine. The sickness she had experienced in Jerusalem had disappeared as they walked along with this man. As she worked preparing a fine lamb stew with lentils, carrots and onions she had grown in her own garden, she listened to the men's conversation about ancient prophecies concerning the Messiah.

When Mary set the pot of stew, a loaf of bread, spoons and bowls on the table, the three were ready to eat. The stranger took the lead, picking up the bread and breaking it in half. He closed his eyes. Clopas and Mary did the same. When He had blessed the bread, they opened their eyes. The voice sounded so familiar and as they looked at Him now, they recognized Jesus. Suddenly He was gone. The couple looked at each other, speechless.

"Did not our heart burn within us while He talked with us on the road?" asked Clopas.

"And while He opened the Scriptures to us?" Mary agreed.

"We must return to Jerusalem and tell the disciples! Do you feel well enough?" Clopas asked.

"Yes, it was like He healed my sick feeling as we listened to Him. We can leave right now." Throwing caution and fatigue aside in the glow of first light, Clopas and Mary went out the door, leaving the meal on the table.

Evening

1 Peter 2:9
But you are a chosen race, a royal priesthood, a holy nation, a people for his own possession, that you may proclaim the excellencies of him who called you out of darkness into his marvelous light.

When the vendors in the marketplace closed their shops and headed home, Jesus' followers gathered again at Mary's house, anxious to hear what Peter and the others had been shown during their prayers.

"No guards came to my shop today or questioned me. Did you have any problem?" asked one of the believers.

"No," came an answer.

"Could Nicodemus have been lying to us so we would play into the Sanhedrin's hands?" asked another.

"I doubt that. He is also a believer," said a merchant.

"At least he appears to be, but he may just be trying to find evidence on us to condemn us."

"Nicodemus is a Pharisee. Why would he 'follow' Jesus?" challenged a woman.

"I heard that he defended Jesus before the Sanhedrin," replied another woman.

"Maybe that was just a story they circulated to make him more believable."

"But he warned us about the possibility of arrest."

"I, too, believe the story of Jesus' resurrection," said Nicodemus as he entered the room.

"Then why have none of us seen any of the Temple Guards today?"

"I can't answer your questions," Nicodemus said. "I was at the Temple all day and heard nothing of the morning meeting. I saw the elders and the High Priest going about their normal activities as if nothing unusual had happened. It was almost like they were purposefully ignoring the event. I didn't even hear a mention of Jesus or the crucifixion."

This answer seemed to satisfy the crowd.

Peter and those who had been in prayer came into the room. When he saw Nicodemus, Peter approached him. The others ceased their discussions to listen.

"Nicodemus, what have you to tell us?" asked Peter.

"Nothing! I have heard absolutely nothing about the tomb or the theft of Jesus' body," he replied. "I know that what I told you is true, but there was no sign of it today. Everything went on just as it always has at the Temple."

"What do you make of it?" Peter pressed.

"The best I can make out is that they have decided to ignore the entire matter in the hope that this whole 'Jesus myth' will be forgotten and with it the threat to them."

"That would make sense," Peter thought aloud. "They may think that, having killed the leader, the followers would scatter and soon there would be nothing more for them to worry about. It has happened before."

Heads nodded in agreement and the hum of human voices began again.

"But," Peter said in a loud voice that immediately drew their attention, "are we going to turn away so quickly from the Messiah? Is not our faith greater than that? Doesn't the resurrection prove that Jesus is the Messiah? Are we going to let Him die? God didn't! Will we?"

The room was silent as everyone considered what Peter was saying. He was challenging their faith. How many of them would return to their previous state of unbelief? And how many would continue in the faith that Jesus is the Messiah? Each one present was making a personal decision. A few quietly slipped out of the house, their decision made. The silence continued for a long time.

"Did you receive an answer to your prayers today? What is God's will for us?" asked a loud voice from the back of the crowd.

"Yes," Peter replied. "The Lord spoke to us. He wants you to return to your daily lives for now, still witnessing for Him to others. Those of you who live in Jerusalem can continue to meet here as we have been doing. Keep your faith in Jesus and share it with others as you have opportunity. Those who live in the outlying villages, should remember what you heard from the Lord's lips and continue to tell others what He said, what you personally know of Him and how believing in Him has changed your life.

"Those of us from Galilee are to return there to await the Lord as the women told us He instructed through the message received this morning. We will leave tomorrow morning, but we will return to you here after He has come to us. Expect us. Above all, believe that Jesus is the Messiah and that He was raised by God from the dead. He is risen!"

The people answered with a resounding "He is risen indeed!"

As excited voices began sharing new plans with each other, there were still a few who harbored doubts. Yet, they lingered, hoping that something would happen to change their hearts and allow them to enthusiastically join the hopeful ones.

The women who had been praying in a separate room heard Peter addressing the growing number of disciples. Mary went to the door to check on her guests.

"It appears that Peter and the others have received the Lord's answer," she told the other women. "Let us help as the servants prepare a meal for those who are here."

The women set about preparations and soon were ready to serve a meal to Mary's guests. Servants cleared tables to hold the food, which was promptly brought out to fill them. There were loaves of bread, apricots, figs, lamb, veal, fish, and a variety of vegetables and sauces. Mary whispered in Peter's ear, telling him that food was ready for those assembled to eat.

"Friends," he said above the din, "Our gracious hostess has provided food for you to eat. Let us thank God for His provision." Mary handed Peter a loaf of bread and he broke it in half. The crowd bowed their heads and Peter continued,

"Blessed art Thou, O Lord our God, who is the gracious Provider of all our needs, we thank you for the food which you have provided for us this evening. Bless it to our bodies and bless the hands which have prepared it. And, most of all, Father, thank you for giving us a risen Savior. We thank You, O God."

As the people partook of the food and wine, Peter and Mary compared the answers each of their groups had received and found them to be in agreement, confirming that what Peter had told the crowd was indeed God's will for them at this time.

Suddenly, a remembrance crossed Peter's mind. He told it to Mary and she handed him another loaf of bread.

"My friends," Peter said loudly. As the crowd quieted, he continued, "On the night of Jesus' arrest, after we had eaten the Passover meal, our Lord took a loaf of bread and as He broke it, He said, 'This is my body which is given for you; take and eat'." Then raising the loaf in his hands, Peter continued.

"Let us follow our Master's instruction and command, beginning now." He broke the loaf, blessed it repeating Jesus' words, took a piece of it and passed the halves both ways into the crowd. Every one took a piece and ate it. Then Peter lifted the cup and said,

"'This is the new covenant in my blood which is shed for you. Drink all of it. As often as you do this, remember Me.'" Peter sipped from the cup and passed it around.

When the rite was complete, the people continued eating the meal and making plans. Then, as the entrance door was opened so some of them could leave, Clopas and Mary excitedly rushed in. Their glowing faces and breathlessness bespoke their hurried journey.

"The Lord has risen indeed! We have seen Him!" Clopas shouted, confirming Mary Magdalene's claim of that morning. "We have walked with Jesus and listened to His teaching. He is alive! He is truly alive!" The crowd surrounded the couple clamoring for details.

"Silence," Peter commanded. When the noise ceased, he turned to Clopas and Mary.

"Tell us all about it," he invited. "Where did you see Him?"

"We had decided to go home this afternoon," Clopas began, the words tumbling out in a constant flow, "because Mary was not feeling well. We were walking along the road discussing what had happened this morning when a stranger joined us. We didn't know who He was. He asked us what we were talking about.

"We told Him about the crucifixion and that Jesus had been raised from the dead. He said we were foolish children. Then He starrted teaching us about the Scriptures which prophesied the Messiah. There were so many – more than we realized. He was so gentle and so wise. We loved hearing him talk and the miles melted away. When we reached our house, we invited Him to eat with us. He came in and continued speaking with us while Mary prepared food. But when He broke the bread and blessed it, our eyes were opened and we recognized Him. It truly was Jesus! Then, suddenly He was gone. We had to come back and tell you the wonderful news. He is alive!"

Praise filled the air! Everyone was singing and dancing and shouting praise to God for His wondrous works.

Suddenly, Jesus himself stood among them. No one noticed Him until He said to them, "Peace to you!"

The dancing stopped and silence filled the room. Most of the people were startled and frightened and thought He was a ghost. As they stared at the Lord, He said to them,

"Why are you troubled, and why do doubts arise in your hearts? See My hands and My feet, that it is I myself. Touch Me, and see. For a spirit does not have flesh and bones as you see that I have." And when He had said this, He showed them His hands and His feet. While they were still marveling and trying to believe what they were witnessing, He continued,

"Have you anything here to eat?" Someone went to the table and handed Him a piece of broiled fish, which He took and ate before them.

Suddenly a festival of rejoicing broke out. The people

sang and danced in celebration. They were so elated that they did not even realize that Jesus was no longer in their midst, leaving as He had arrived. The celebration continued far into the night as the people expressed their joy and exulted in their now solid belief that Jesus had risen from the dead, leaving no doubt that He is God's Son. When they were finally exhausted, they returned to their homes.

As the last followers left, the eleven disciples of Jesus' inner circle said goodnight to Mary and John Mark and returned to their rented room for some rest and to prepare for their journey back to Galilee in the morning.

Epilogue

Matthew 5:16
In the same way, let your light shine before others, so that they may see your good works and give glory to your Father who is in heaven.

And so the disciples returned to Galilee to await Jesus. James, the Lord's brother, Matthew, Nathaniel and Bartholomew, Jesus' disciples, remained in Jerusalem to encourage the followers as they witnessed for Jesus. Peter and Andrew with James and John, the sons of Zebedee, returned to fishing.

There was comfort in working the nets and the gentle rocking of the boat. They had missed this occupation, and they knew within themselves that when they left it again, there would be no returning – ever.

The time they now had with family was also cherished as a treasure that would soon be lost. John remembered how Jesus had told the teacher who wanted to follow Him that "Foxes have holes and birds of the air have nests, but the Son of Man has nowhere to lay His head." Having followed Him these three years, the disciples well understood that truth. They didn't know what Jesus would ask of them, but they were ready to obey whatever He commanded.

Some time had passed since the Galileans left Jerusalem. Yesterday several of the disciples, Thomas, Philip, Simon and James, the son of Alphaeus, had come to talk with Peter and the others. They were all wondering when Jesus would come to them as He had promised. With evening approaching, the visitors had accepted the fishermen's invitation to go fishing with them that night. So Zebedee's boat on the Sea of Galilee was where they were in the early morning, coming in from a fishless night. But this time, it didn't seem to matter. The fellowship of these men was strengthening them. They did not know what lay ahead, but they were all at peace with whatever it would be.

As the sun peeked over the hills, they came past a small beach several miles south of their home in Capernaum. There was a figure standing near a small fire on the shore.

"Children, have you any food?" he called to them.

"No," they answered.

"Cast the net on the right side of the boat, and you will find some," the man replied.

"Go ahead," Peter casually told Andrew, "Cast it on the right side."

Andrew threw the net. When the weights had settled, the men began to haul it in. They knew immediately that the haul was big and as they tugged on it, John remarked that he hoped the nets would hold. Suddenly, he remembered another time and a similar experience. He looked more closely at the man on the shore and recognized Jesus.

"It's the Lord!" John exclaimed. Upon hearing this, Peter threw off his tunic, plunged into the water and began swimming toward shore.

His astounded companions finished hauling the net

into the boat and immediately turned toward the shore. When they reached the beach, Peter was embracing his Lord.

Although the nets held more than one hundred fifty fish, miraculously, they were still intact.

"Bring some of the fish you have just caught" Jesus said. They saw a fire of coals laid under some fish and a loaf of bread on a nearby stone.

"Come and eat breakfast," He invited. Removing the cooked fish, He handed them to those standing near the fire and laid the newly caught fish on the coals to cook. Joy and celebration followed as the group ate the fish and bread.

While the other disciples were eating, Jesus drew Peter aside. The two walked a short distance from the beach where they could speak privately. Peter couldn't help but wonder why the Lord wanted to talk with him alone. *Is Jesus disappointed with me because His prediction proved true? I did deny Him the night of His arrest. Or, worse yet, is He angry with me? I well deserve punishment!* Peter revisited the bitterness he experienced in Jerusalem over his actions.

When they came to a fallen tree, Jesus sat down and bade Peter to sit beside Him. Jesus looked at him and smiled. *He doesn't appear to be angry.* Peter relaxed a bit. They both looked at a beetle crawling onto a large stone at their feet. When Jesus put His hand on Peter's arm, their eyes met.

"Simon, son of Jonah, do you love Me more than these?" He asked gesturing toward the rest of the disciples, the water, the fish and bread.

"Yes, Lord," he answered, "You know that I love You."

"Feed My lambs," He replied. Silence filled the air for a long minute. Jesus looked out over the Sea of Galilee before turning again to Peter's now tear-filled eyes.

"Simon, son of Jonah, do you love Me?" Jesus asked again. Peter was puzzled. *Doesn't Jesus know the depth of my love? How could He ask this question again? Perhaps my denial has shaken the Lord's opinion of me. Did I destroy the Master's trust in me? I showed that I was all bluster, not substance, in my denial of Him. But that is not me! I truly love Him and will prove it if it takes the rest of my life!*

"Yes, Lord, You know that I love You," he answered in a choked voice that betrayed his anguish.

"Tend My sheep," Jesus said. After another long silence watching the beetle's progress, Jesus spoke again.

"Simon, son of Jonah, do you love Me?" Now Peter was angry because Jesus kept asking him the same question.

"Lord, You know all things. You know that I love You," he exploded as he stood and faced his Master.

"Feed My sheep," Jesus calmly told him as He stood and put His hand on Peter's shoulder. "Most assuredly, I say to you, when you were younger, you girded yourself and walked where you wished, but when you are old, you will stretch out your hands and another will gird you and carry you where you do not wish." Jesus squarely faced Peter and held out His hand to him. "Follow Me." Peter took Jesus' hand and they walked back to the group on the beach.

Peter did not fully understand what Jesus had meant by this exchange, but later he would realize that Jesus had been commissioning him for the work he would do for the rest of his life. He was now ready to do this work the way the Lord wanted him to do it. If he hadn't experienced his own failures of faith, he would not understand the people to whom he would witness in the coming years. Now he could approach them in the same humility his Savior had demonstrated during the Passover meal when He washed the disciples' feet.

All of them had been appalled when the Master left the table at the end of the meal. By the door was a stand where water, a basin and towel had been placed to wash the guests' feet from the grime of the road. No one had yet performed that task, but Jesus calmly, without a word, walked to the table, girded Himself with the towel filled the basin and picked it up.

He first approached Judas Iscariot, who was at one end of the table. Silently, He kneeled, placed the basin next to the couch and gently moved the man's feet down to the basin. Taking one foot at a time, the Lord held the foot above the basin and splashed water onto it, working the grime out from between his toes with His fingers. Then cupping His hand, He gathered water and poured it over the foot, rinsing the dirt off. Tenderly, he dried the foot with the towel and returned it to its place on the couch. After washing the other foot, Jesus moved the basin to the disciple sitting next to Judas and repeated the procedure.

Jesus worked His way down the table while the disciples looked on in confused awe. Then He reached Peter, who could stand it no longer! When Jesus began to kneel next to his couch, Peter jumped to his feet.

"Lord, are You washing my feet?" he asked incredulously.

"What I am doing you do not understand now, but you will know after this," Jesus calmly answered.

"You shall never wash my feet!" Peter blustered defiantly.

"If I do not wash you," Jesus quietly replied, "you have no part of Me."

Peter's countenance changed to one of confusion. He looked at the other disciples, but they just looked back at him in awestruck silence.

"Lord, not my feet only, but also my hands and my

163

head," he cried out, his hands reaching toward Jesus, imploring.

"He who is bathed needs only to wash his feet, but is completely clean and you are clean," Jesus answered. Then He looked around the assembly and added, "but you are not all clean."

Dumbstruck and puzzled, Peter sat back down on the couch and Jesus knelt and washed his feet, then moved to John. When all of the disciples' feet were clean, Jesus removed the towel and placed it with the basin back on the table. Returning to His place at the main table, Jesus addressed them.

"Do you know what I have done to you?" He began. "You call me Teacher and Lord, and you say well, for so I am. If I then, your Lord and Teacher, have washed your feet, you also ought to wash one another's feet, for I have given you an example, that you should do as I have done to you."

Recalling this event, Peter was beginning to understand. *Jesus wants me to be a gentle leader, as God is – loving others more than myself. I know I failed my Lord in denying Him, but now I know that I am forgiven. Jesus made me finally understand not only what He wants from me, but the manner in which I am to live the rest of my life.* Jesus had also foretold Peter how he would die. Before that time came, however, he and the rest of the disciples had much work to do. Jesus entrusted these men with the most important mission in the world, the spreading of the good news of God's love, as exemplified by the earthly journey of His Son.

The disciples were now His Apostles. They had been just ordinary people doing ordinary work, but one day each of them met Jesus and they were transformed – their lives totally changed.

Hope for all the world was redeemed when the Lord Jesus arose and exited the grave. This was the message to be carried by these apostles to all the world – to transform the lives of millions of people over twenty centuries. The good news of Jesus' love for sinners has brought God's first light to the world – hope that transcends the centuries and transforms the lives of all who believe and accept it.

In the intervening years, one-by-one, these men met their Master, always in God's service and filled with the Holy Spirit who dwelt in them. They were faithful shepherds who established God's love in the hearts and souls of those who came to know Jesus because of their teaching, writing and witness – and the teaching and witness of those who followed them. The Lord's nets are full today because they decided to accept Jesus' invitation to become "fishers of men."

Lives are still being transformed.

Is yours one of them?

Hebrews 13:15
Through him then let us continually offer up a sacrifice of praise to God, that is, the fruit of lips that acknowledge his name.

Ephesians 5:8
For at one time you were darkness, but now you are light in the Lord. Walk as children of light.

First Light

Death has a darkness
    All its own.
        No life in the flesh.
            No life in the bone.
All seems so hopeless.
    All seems to be lost,
        And those who are mourning
            Are counting the cost.
But all is not dead!
    All is not gone!
        The grave will not win!
            Life will go on!

For when darkest night
    Gives way to dawn,
        Hope is restored,
            Hearts are reborn!
Healed hearts are singing
    In bright midday sun.
        Celebrating forever
            The victory won!
No pain, no worry,
    Only Peace from above –
        First light in His Son
            Of God's perfect love.

Scripture References

Because this is a Biblically-based novel, these scripture references are provided as a guide to the quotations of the words of Jesus as found in the English Standard Version of the Holy Bible.

Prologue
  Matthew 21:13

Part I

Simon Peter, the Rock
  Mark 1:21-34
  Luke 5:1-9
  Luke 22:31-34
  Luke 22:55-62
  Matthew 14:22-33
  Matthew 16:22-28

John, the Beloved
  Matthew 17:1-13
  John 16:20

Andrew, the Gatherer
  Mark 10:13-16
  John 6:1-14
  Matthew 7:4-5

Matthew, the Publican
  Matthew 6:16, 19-21; 24, 26-34
  Mark 2:13-17

Simon, the Zealot
  Luke 14:1-11
  Luke 19:42-44
  John 13:21-27
  Matthew 27:3-5

Mary Magdala, the Rescued
  Luke 6:35, 37
  Luke 8:2,3
  Psalm 27:10
  Luke 24:33-43

Nicodemus, the Pharisee
  John 3:1-21
  John 7:45-52

Mark, the Seeker
  Luke 6:47-49
  Matthew 13:10-17

James, the Brother of Jesus
  John 2:1-10
  Luke 4:16-29
  Matthew 12:47-50
  John 19:26, 27

Part II

Dawn
  Mark 16:1-8
  Matthew 28:1-8
  John 20:11-18
  Matthew 28:11-15
  John 20:1-10

Morning
  Matthew 28:11-15
  John 20:1-10
  Matthew 26:31, 32
  Mark 14:27, 28

Evening
  Luke 24:13-32

Epilogue
  John 21:1-19
  John 13:1-15

Bibliography of Sources

Holy Bible – English Standard Version

Barclay, William, *"The Daily Study Bible Series,"* Philadelphia, PA, The Westminster Press, 1971.

Edersheim, Alfred, *"The Life and Times of Jesus the Messiah: New Updated Edition,"* Peabody, MA, Hendrickson Publishers, Inc., 1993.

Edersheim, Alfred, *"Sketcher of Jewish Social Life."* Peabody, MA, Hendrickson Publishers, Inc., 1994.

Gardner, Joseph L., Editor, *"Atlas of the Bible,"* Pleasantville, NY. Reader's Digest Association, Inc., 1981.

Lockyer, Sr., Herbert, General Editor, *"Nelson's Illustrated Bible Dictionary,"* Nashville, TN, Thomas Nelson Publishers, 1986.

Morison, Frank, *"Who Moved the Stone?"* Grand Rapids, MI, Zondervan, 1958.

Packer, J. I. and Tenney, M. C., Editors, *"Illustrated Manners and Customs of the Bible,"* Nashville, TN, Thomas Nelson Publishers, 1980.

"The Bethel Series – New Testament", Madison, WI, Adult Christian Education Foundation, 1961.

Ward, Kaari, Editor, *"Jesus and His Times,"* Pleasantville, NY, Reader's Digest Association, Inc.,1987.

About the Author

Carolyn Gilliam, a graduate of the University of Wichita with a major in English, always wanted to write books. "Two trips to Israel brought the Bible to life for me and I found my voice," she says.

Her fictional accounts of Bible events and down- to-earth characters gleaned from years of teaching classes and diligent research, give both seekers and seasoned saints with new perspectives on their lives.

Carolyn lives in Missouri with an active family and four love-sponge Havanese dogs.

A free Bible Study for this book is available at: carolyngilliam.com

Reach Carolyn at: cgilliam@carolyngilliam.com.

Another Book by Carolyn Gilliam

From Mourning Into Gladness

Life is good for young Rachel and her family. But her children are murdered, and for the next thirty years, she is plagued with a question most people ask at one time or another. "Why?"

When a series of unexpected events takes her behind the scenes of one of history's greatest tragedies and she finds new meaning to her life, freedom from her past and hope for the future.

Join Rachel, her husband Eli, and family in this heart-wrenching-to-heart-warming journey from sorrow into joy.

www.ingramcontent.com/pod-product-compliance
Lightning Source LLC
Chambersburg PA
CBHW061649040426
42446CB00010B/1654